# Haunted Houses

Fact or Fiction?

# Haunted Houses

# Other books in the Fact or Fiction? series:

# Haunted Houses

Fact or Fiction?

Terry O'Neill, *Book Editor*

Daniel Leone, *President*
Bonnie Szumski, *Publisher*
Scott Barbour, *Managing Editor*

OPPOSING
VIEWPOINTS®
SERIES

GREENHAVEN
PRESS®

THOMSON
─────✳─────
GALE

San Diego • Detroit • New York • San Francisco • Cleveland
New Haven, Conn. • Waterville, Maine • London • Munich

LIBRARY OF CONGRESS CATALOGING-IN-PUBLICATION DATA

Haunted houses / Terry O'Neill, book editor.
   p. cm. — (Fact or fiction?)
Includes bibliographical references and index.
ISBN 0-7377-1068-3 (lib. : alk. paper) — ISBN 0-7377-1067-5 (pbk. : alk. paper)
   1. Haunted houses. I. O'Neill, Terry, 1944– . II. Fact or fiction? (Greenhaven Press)
BF1475.H32  2004
133.1'22—dc21
                                     2003054025

# Contents

# Foreword

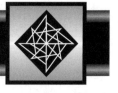

"There are more things in heaven and earth, Horatio, than are dreamt of in your philosophy."
—William Shakespeare, *Hamlet*

"Extraordinary claims require extraordinary evidence."
—Carl Sagan, *The Demon-Haunted World*

Almost every one of us has experienced something that we thought seemed mysterious and unexplainable. For example, have you ever known that someone was going to call you just before the phone rang? Or perhaps you have had a dream about something that later came true. Some people think these occurrences are signs of the paranormal. Others explain them as merely coincidence.

As the examples above show, mysteries of the paranormal ("beyond the normal") are common. For example, most towns have at least one place where inhabitants believe ghosts live. People report seeing strange lights in the sky that they believe are the spaceships of visitors from other planets. And scientists have been working for decades to discover the truth about sightings of mysterious creatures like Bigfoot and the Loch Ness monster.

There are also mysteries of magic and miracles. The two often share a connection. Many forms of magical belief are tied to religious belief. For example, many of the rituals and beliefs of the voodoo religion are viewed by outsiders as magical practices. These include such things as the alleged Haitian voodoo practice of turning people into zombies (the walking dead).

There are mysteries of history—events and places that have been recorded in history but that we still have questions about today. For example, was the great King Arthur a real king or merely a legend? How, exactly, were the pyramids built? Historians continue to seek the answers to these questions.

Then, of course, there are mysteries of science. One such mystery is how humanity began. Although most scientists agree that it was through the long, slow process of evolution, not all scientists agree that indisputable proof has been found.

Subjects like these are fascinating, in part because we do not know the whole truth about them. They are mysteries. And they are controversial—people hold very strong and opposing views about them.

How we go about sifting through information on such topics is the subject of every book in the Greenhaven Press series Fact or Fiction? Each anthology includes articles that present the main ideas favoring and challenging a given topic. The editor collects such material from a variety of sources, including scientific research, eyewitness accounts, and government reports. In addition, a final chapter gives readers tools to analyze the articles they read. With these tools, readers can sift through the information presented in the articles by applying the methods of hypothetical reasoning. Examining these topics in this way adds a unique aspect to the Fact or Fiction? series. Hypothetical reasoning can be applied to any topic to allow a reader to become more analytical about the material he or she encounters. While such reasoning may not solve the mystery of who is right or who is wrong, it can help the reader separate valid from invalid evidence relating to all topics and can be especially helpful in analyzing material where people disagree.

# Introduction

Every town has one. A deserted, rundown old house on a hilltop or deep in the woods. Occasionally passersby report seeing a light or a mysterious figure peering from a window. Young people dare each other to spend the night there. And rumors abound. A vicious ghost is said to haunt this place.

But not all haunted houses fit this stereotype. If we broaden the term to include various kinds of human dwellings, haunted houses span an amazing range of types. Here are a few of the more than two thousand "haunts" reported by Dennis William Hauck in his *National Directory of Haunted Houses:*

- Bolivar, Tennessee: A former owner's ghost is seen rocking on the front porch of the quaint, old Parran house.
- Honolulu, Hawaii: The spirit of a young girl dressed in white makes appearances near a fountain at Iolani Palace.
- Wilmington, North Carolina: Confederate general William Whiting's ghost haunts the ruins of Fort Fisher.
- Minneapolis, Minnesota: Patrons and employees of the Guthrie Theater have seen the ghost of a former usher who took his own life while working there.
- West Palm Beach, Florida: Employees at a Burger King on U.S. Highway 1 report that they have chased the ghost that haunts this fast-food joint.
- New Orleans, Louisiana: Visitors to the Beauregard-Keyes house say that on some nights at 2:00 A.M. the

ballroom turns into a ghostly Civil War battleground.
• Washington, D.C.: The White House is said to be home
  to several ghosts, including that of Abraham Lincoln.

As this brief list shows, haunted houses come in all sizes
and varieties—a haunted house may be a dark and decrepit
old place, but it might also be a sparkling new townhouse,
a mansion, a boat, a fort, a school—or a Burger King! But
what qualifies a house or other edifice as "haunted"? Of
the haunted places listed in Hauck's book, only a few have
been seriously investigated. Most are simply described as
haunted by the people who live in the area because of
strange events that occur there. Sometimes people report
seeing apparitions, but sometimes the only symptoms of a
haunting are strange lights or noises; no ghost is ever actually seen by anyone. Most haunted houses seem to be
called that because someone—or maybe several people—
have reported having strange experiences there and the
place's reputation has stuck.

Those who believe in hauntings often distinguish between the types of entity that haunt a place. The most common hauntings are supposedly caused by ghosts, poltergeists, or demons.

## Haunting by a Ghost

Most haunted houses are believed to be haunted by ghosts,
most commonly defined as spirits of the dead. Often the
person whose spirit is said to haunt a place is known. In the
Bolivar, Tennessee, example above, townspeople knew old
Dave Parran. In his later years (he died at age eighty-six), he
spent most days sitting on his porch greeting and chatting
with passersby. So townspeople conclude that the ghost that
some people report seeing sitting on the porch is Dave Parran's spirit.

Sometimes the ghost is unknown. For example, no one

really knows who the Burger King ghost might have been when alive.

Sometimes a place is haunted not by a single ghost but by a whole gaggle of ghosts who may be completely unrelated or may be connected in a strange, spectral tableau. For example, Abe Lincoln is only one of several ghosts that are said to haunt the White House, and at the Beauregard-Keyes house, General Beauregard rides through the ballroom doors on his white horse while legions of phantom soldiers battle, eventually falling, moaning, and crying out for help.

Ghosts are thought to make themselves apparent in several ways. At Fredericksburg, Virginia, two common ghostly manifestations occur—the ghost of a heroic soldier bringing water to his dying comrades is *seen*, and the sounds of the other soldiers are *heard*. Examples of other spectral manifestations include smells (the aroma of the perfume a woman was known to have worn in life or the smell of a cigar even though no smoker is present); lights (misty orbs, moving pinpoints, glowing candle flames); sounds (talking, creaks, the sounds of doors slamming); drafts or winds; cold spots or sudden drops in temperature; and objects moved or thrown.

## Haunting by a Poltergeist

A poltergeist is also called a mischievous spirit or a noisy ghost, but parapsychologists (people who study things beyond the bounds of the normal world) say that poltergeists generally have no known connection to a dead person. In fact, they are usually attached in some way to a living person—their manifestations usually occur when a particular person is present, or their activities are focused on a particular person. Poltergeists tend to be noisy and mischievous. They throw, drop, and break things; turn lights on and off; and move objects, even making them float through the air.

Some poltergeists have been reported to scratch people or pull their hair. They cause a disturbance.

Michael White, author of *Weird Science: An Expert Explains Ghosts, Voodoo, the UFO Conspiracy, and Other Paranormal Phenomena*, distinguishes between ghosts and poltergeists this way: "Apparitions [ghosts] are largely *passive*, whereas poltergeists are *active*. Apparitions are usually witnessed as images, which impart information or respond to living beings only rarely, whereas poltergeists are frequently reported to interact with the living."[1]

## Haunting by a Demon

Some people believe a demon is an evil kind of spiritual entity that is generally not connected to any particular dead person. A demon may do some of the things a poltergeist does but to a much stronger, more malevolent extent. It may try to possess or take over a living person's personality. It may cause great harm.

## The Investigators and Their Methods

Keep in mind that just because people say a house is haunted does not mean it really is. When haunted houses are examined using sound investigative methods, most of them are found to have an explanation that does not include ghosts. Some of the more common explanations will be discussed later in this introduction.

Investigations of haunted houses are usually done by a parapsychologist. Some parapsychologists have advanced academic degrees and many years of experience as scientists. Some have been private or police investigators. Some consider themselves to be psychic.

Sometimes more mainstream scientists investigate haunted houses, but the paranormal field has limited interest to many scientists who believe that such subjects cannot be successfully studied using true scientific methods. They also tend to believe that there is not enough evidence to prove that ghosts actually exist. Some scientists who may have a personal interest in this topic believe they will harm their careers or their scientific credibility if they participate in the investigation of haunted houses. The result is that there are far more amateur or psychic haunted house investigators than scientific ones. Yet many ghost investigators make every effort to take a scientific approach to their investigations.

The most common types of haunted house investigations might be described as psychic, scientific, and a combination of the two.

## Psychic Investigation

A person with psychic abilities is thought to be able to communicate with other people or with spirits through mental communication. An older term for a psychic who communicates with spirits is *medium* because this person acts as an intermediary between the human and spirit worlds. Mediums have been communicating with spirits for eons. In the late nineteenth century, when a movement arose to try to prove the existence of ghosts, mediums were most often the only means used: If a medium could contact a spirit (as evidenced by table rappings, apparition appearances, and other phenomena), then that was proof that the spirit existed. Naturally, there were frauds, but the Society for Psychical Research, an important organization with members in the scientific community, made every effort to weed out the frauds. Today, some scientists are using more modern and sophisticated means to try to verify psychic ability, but on the whole, belief in a person's mediumistic ability is a matter of faith rather than science.

So how is a psychic investigation of a supposedly haunted

house conducted? Two approaches are common. In one, the psychic interviews the inhabitants of a haunted house and other witnesses. The psychic finds out what kinds of phenomena have occurred and where they have occurred. When examining the house, the psychic pays special attention to the areas where phenomena have occurred before. In the second approach, the psychic goes to the place "cold"—that is, he or she avoids learning anything at all about the types of phenomena or places they have occurred. The psychic tours the house trying to discover any unusual phenomena. Then he or she compares what was discovered with what the homeowners say they have experienced. In both cases, the psychic visits the house and gathers impressions.

In any haunted house investigation, of course, the investigators hope to witness the phenomena firsthand, but this often does not happen; ghosts are not on call, so sometimes a psychic impression of an unusual energy is the strongest evidence that can be found.

Generally the psychic makes an effort to communicate with any ghost or other spiritual entity he or she senses. Such communication, which may take place when the psychic is in a trance, can add additional information to support the existence of a ghost. For example, the psychic may be able to find out personal or historical information from the ghost that can later be checked through public and private records. If the information turns out to be true, it can lend credence to the ghost's existence. Some people believe a psychic's communication with a ghost can also reveal an effective way to help the phantom leave the site of its haunting. For example, if the psychic discovers that the ghost is that of a murdered person who remains connected to the house by its desperate longing for recognition or justice, sometimes simply revealing the ghost's story to the public may provide the closure the spirit needs before it can depart the earthly plane.

As convincing as psychic communication is to some people, keep in mind that most scientists will not accept the results of a psychic investigation as worthwhile evidence of a ghost. Scientists generally want a more concrete kind of evidence.

## Scientific Investigation

Today, many sophisticated, affordable instruments are available for ghost investigators to use to try to obtain concrete evidence, but this was not always the case. Then, in the 1960s, Gertrude Schmeidler, psychology professor at City University of New York, devised a statistical method for investigating a haunting. She mapped a supposedly haunted house, indicating all rooms. Then she interviewed the occupants. She marked on the map every place they had experienced something relating to the haunting. She also made a list of the words they used to describe their experience.

The next step was to gather participants. She enlisted several people who thought they were psychic and several who thought they were not. Without telling them anything about the house or its occupants, she had them tour it. On blank maps they marked any place they felt something "haunting," and they described the feelings they had about these spots.

Finally, she analyzed all the maps and word lists to find out what statistical correlation there was between what the house's occupants experienced and what the participants experienced on their visit. A statistically significant correlation could indicate a haunting—or at least that something unusual was going on in the house. This technique was considered an important breakthrough in haunted house investigations because it relied on more than the impressions of a single psychic.

Today, the first step that scientific "ghost hunters" take is to do as much preliminary investigation as they can to eliminate as many conceivable natural explanations as possible. For example, they try to find out whether a "haunted" house is sitting on a ground fault or is located over an underground water stream (both of which could cause vibrations, noises, and other effects), whether doors and windows are draft-free and closed securely, and how close the house is to electrical lines. All of these—and other factors— can cause effects that seem like ghostly manifestations. Investigators also look for evidence of hoaxing. Then they visit the house, often several times, and they use various instruments to capture anomalies that might be indicative of a ghost—such things as unexplained, sudden temperature changes, images showing up on photos or videotape that were not visible to the investigators when they were filming, proof that objects have moved with no apparent cause, and so on. Most use many scientific instruments in their investigations. These include ordinary instruments like thermometers, cameras, tape recorders, and video cameras, as well as more sophisticated tools such as radiation and electromagnetic detectors, infrared film, and thermal imagers.

In 2001 British paranormal investigator Richard Wiseman conducted one of the largest ghost investigations ever. Along with some professional colleagues and about two hundred public volunteers, he investigated the reputedly haunted dungeons of Edinburgh Castle in Edinburgh, Scotland. Wiseman and his crew combined Schmeidler's mapping technique with the use of a thermal imager, geomagnetic sensors, video and still cameras, temperature probes, night-vision devices, and other high-tech equipment. According to Wiseman, "We and the volunteers were unaware of the [specific] history of the vaults [dungeons], but the volunteers reported experiences more often in the vaults reputed to be most haunted. . . . Whatever the explanation, it means that there is something going on because otherwise we would expect the distribution [of incidents] to have been more random."[2]

So far, no scientific ghost hunter has captured absolutely incontrovertible evidence that a house is haunted, but several investigators, including Wiseman, have discovered unexplainable anomalies that are suggestive of ghosts or some unknown entity.

## Combination Investigation

Many haunted house investigators use a combination of the previous two methods: They use scientific instruments, but they also include at least one psychic in the investigation crew. They hope that psychic impressions will back up anomalies caught by their scientific tools.

## How Investigators Explain Ghostly Phenomena

Sometimes investigators think that they have found slight or impressive evidence of a ghost. But scientists say that most spectral evidence can have other explanations. Here are some common explanations for ghostly phenomena:

*Natural phenomena.* Creaks, moans, strange air drafts, and cold spots can sometimes be explained by a house's settling, underground water streams, and earth vibrations, among other things. Ghostly lights can be caused by reflections, ground fog, or electrical effects.

*Mind tricks.* It is easy to be fooled by an optical illusion, misinterpretation of an experience, or preconceived ideas. For example, either consciously or unconsciously, people going into a supposedly haunted house may be expecting to experience a ghost, so they are quick to assume that a sound or a vague visual impression is a ghost.

Skeptical scientists Dorion Sagan and Jessica Whiteside provide another example:

The creaking of heated houses with the coming of night (the time of ghosts) is associated with an increase in temperature gradient from inside the house to outdoors. Streamers of warmer air (more likely to contain vaguely visible dust in older houses) can be expected to head toward the exits during such times. If viewed fleetingly by people, they could occasionally be sensed both tactilely and visually as ghosts. (The supposed ability to morph through a keyhole is also consonant with this view.) Indeed, those who insulate houses, broadcasting fine powders into the air in order to see its subtle movements, sometimes witness exceedingly "purposeful" movements: a given parcel of warm air may even "change its mind," going up a wall, across a ceiling, and down an opposite wall, only to reverse directions back whence it came, to head through the spaces of an electric outlet.[3]

*Hallucination.* Ghostly hallucinations can be caused by serious mental or physical conditions like schizophrenia, epilepsy, and drug use. They can also be caused by mental or physical exhaustion and sleep deprivation.

Even a person in fine physical and mental health can seem to experience phantoms while in the state between sleep and waking. Robert Novella, cofounder of the New England Skeptic Society, writes,

Hypnagogia . . . occurs when one is waking up (hypnapompic) or going to sleep (hypnagogic). It is an in-between state where one is neither fully awake nor fully asleep. In this state very realistic images and sounds can be experienced. Although visual and auditory hallucinations are most common, experiences can range from hearing your name whispered to ones involving all the senses, including touch. They are in essence dream experiences that are occurring while you are awake.[4]

*Hoax.* People love to play tricks on one another, especially if they achieve a few moments of fame in the process. Many a haunted house has turned out to be the product of a simple or sophisticated hoax. Donald Trull, editor of the now-defunct website Parascope.com, told about a poignant ghost hoax. A young family was experiencing a ghost or poltergeist that manifested itself primarily through the television, telephone, and other electronic devices, even going so far as to change the family's bank card PIN (personal identification number). The ghost called itself Sommy and interrupted phone calls with grunting and burping sounds and threatening messages. Trull reports that "police, private investigators, surveillance crews, and officials from Bell Canada were unable to identify the source of the disturbances." *Dateline NBC* even reported on the strange case. Some people had suspicions about the family's fifteen-year-old son (teenagers are often the pranksters in "poltergeist" cases), but his parents were convinced of his innocence. In fact, they were about to take him to the police and make an official statement to that effect. Then the boy confessed. What had started out as a practical joke with his friends soon "completely grew out of control until he didn't know how to stop."[5]

## Dealing with a Haunted House

If people believe their house is truly haunted, there are a number of things they can do.

*Expose it.* Those who prefer not to live with ghostly phenomena may choose to do a thorough investigation, possibly with an expert's help, to discover if there are natural explanations that can be dealt with. For example, if the ghost that opens and closes doors turns out to be a draft from a crack in a door or wall, the crack can be patched, and the "ghost" is no more.

*Live with it.* Some people choose to continue living with the "ghost." Most of those who live in haunted houses find that the spirits are benign. If anything, they are more of a nuisance than a danger, and some find them companionable. Typical of this perspective is a young British couple who was experiencing various strange goings-on in their apartment.

They brought in an investigation team to find out the source of their problems, and the team concluded that the place was haunted by a country gentleman, a collie dog, and a young girl with breathing problems, probably because she had died in a fire in the building many years before. Once the couple had an explanation, they refused to try to get rid of the ghosts. "I might miss them if they were gone," the woman said. "They have become part of our lives."[6]

*Wait it out.* In the case of a poltergeist and some ghosts, the homeowner may just want to wait it out. Poltergeists, in particular, usually "haunt" a house for a relatively short period—weeks or a few months. So if the disturbances are bearable and can be ignored, they may very well go away on their own.

*Send it to the light.* If the homeowner wants to get rid of a ghost, he or she can try to send it to the light—that is, tell it to stop lingering on Earth and move on to the afterlife where it belongs. (Many people believe that when a person dies, his or her spirit ascends to the afterlife through a tunnel that leads to a tremendously bright spiritual light.) Rosemary Ellen Guiley, author of *The Encyclopedia of Ghosts and Spirits*, writes,

> In contemporary spirit releasement, a practitioner . . . makes contact with a spirit who is haunting a site. . . . Often this is an earthbound soul who does not know he or she is dead, or is bound to the earth plane by unfinished business.

> Practitioners say that simply finding out the entity's "story," that is, its life and death and perhaps unfinished business, is often sufficient to send the spirit on its way to the next world. The entity is engaged in dialogue and persuaded to depart. . . . [But] sometimes the earthbound spirit has to be convinced to move on.[7]

*Exorcise it.* A homeowner who believes the house is haunted by a demon will have to take more drastic measures. He or she can hire a demonologist or consult with a Catholic priest or other practitioner about performing an exorcism, a religious ceremony designed to rid a place of a demon.

## Real Hauntings?

So, are haunted houses really haunted? According to a 2001 Gallup poll, about 30 percent of Americans believe they are. Even the nation's courts have sometimes seemed to concur. On more than one occasion, a house sale has been voided by the courts because the seller neglected to mention that the home housed a ghost. "We were victims of ectoplasmic fraud,"[8] asserted one successful complainant. (Ectoplasm is a filmy substance that is said to materialize at some séances and that some people believe is what ghosts are made of.)

Still, most scientists remain skeptical. There has yet to be a haunting case in which scientists have agreed with parapsychologists about its genuineness. Until such a case appears, people will have to examine the evidence and decide for themselves.

## Notes

1. Michael White, *Weird Science: An Expert Explains Ghosts, Voodoo, the UFO Conspiracy, and Other Paranormal Phenomena.* New York: Avon, 1999, p. 117.
2. Quoted in *BBC News*, "Scientists Report Ghostly Goings-On," April 16, 2001. http://news.bbc.co.uk.
3. Dorion Sagan and Jessica Whiteside, "A Skeptical View of 'The Sciences of Complexity,'" *SWIFT, Online Newsletter of the JREF* (James Randi Educational Foundation), January 25, 2002. www.randi.org.
4. Robert Novella, "Hypnagogia," *Connecticut Skeptic,* vol. 1, no. 2, Spring 1996, p. 3.
5. Donald Trull, "Electronic Possession." http://web.archive.org.
6. Quoted in "Fire Explains Ghostly Guests," *This Is Hampshire*, April 16, 2003. www.thisishampshire.net.
7. Rosemary Ellen Guiley, "Spirit Releasement," in *The Encyclopedia of Ghosts and Spirits.* 2nd ed. New York: Facts On File, 2000, p. 360.
8. Tim Madigan, "Caveat Specter," *Skeptical Briefs*, June 1995. www.csicop.org.

# Chapter 1

**Fact or Fiction?**

# Evidence for
# Haunted Houses

# How to Tell If a House Is Haunted

Patricia Telesco

Most people associate haunted houses with strange sounds and unusual lights and shadows. However, there are other phenomena that indicate a house is haunted. In the following viewpoint, author Patricia Telesco describes common signs that a house is haunted. She is careful to point out that these signs often have more ordinary explanations—or even nonghostly paranormal ones. She mentions "false faces," which she defines elsewhere as spiritual entities or energies that appear or that interact with humans much like ghosts do but are not ghosts (spirits of the deceased). Only after "false faces" and natural causes have been ruled out should a person begin to think that a ghost or poltergeist may be present.

Telesco has written many books and articles on paranormal topics, including *The Language of Dreams, Future Telling,* and *Folkways: Reclaiming the Magic and Wisdom.*

How do we know that a house, area, or object is haunted? It's not easy. There can be natural causes for the events and activities reported in a haunting. Swamp gas and floaters [cells that leak into the eye's vitreous liquid and look like circles or strings floating in front of the eye] might explain an odd visual image. Wind, a settling house, or a playful pet may be responsible for spooky noises. Or the spiritual entity you encounter may be a "false face." So what's a layperson ghost hunter to do?

When you first suspect the presence of a ghost, begin immediately to maintain detailed records. Later on, these may help verify or disprove a haunting, with the aid of experts. Records should include the following entries.

- Date, time, and duration of each incident, along with a detailed description of what happened.
- Sound recordings, photographs, or video recordings, if the equipment is available.
- A description of the prevalent environmental factors, including the weather, and any people or pets present.
- Names and addresses of any witnesses, and their own narratives of what they experienced. . . .

If you cherish specific expectations, these may create a self-induced experience. Suppose a child is afraid that monsters lurk in the dark. Upon going to bed, the child is likely to think he or she sees one in the shadows, or to dream of monsters. Adults are not immune to such imaginings. One night, after reading about ghosts, I looked into a darkened room—and saw an odd, etheric glow. My heart began to race, and I tried desperately to find my camera. But I found, when I examined the room closely, that the glow came from moonlight, reflecting off a crystal on the windowsill. Skepticism is your ally when you catalogue apparently ghostly phenomena.

## Indications That a Home or Object Is Haunted

Objects or homes can be haunted by a spirit attached to them. A ghost can develop a very strong emotional attachment to a place, or an item—usually one it owned or coveted during life. When the attachment is so intense that it hinders a spirit's transition into the next life, the object is called a "fetter." You can tell whether there is a fetter by examining the symptoms the environment or object exhibits.

To help you refine your investigation, I have provided a list of common symptoms of hauntings. These entries will help you determine whether you are dealing with a *ghost*. A "false face," or a natural phenomenon, will exhibit different symptoms, which are discussed in the "Skeptical Advisor" sections.

## Aroma

Distinct scents wafting through the home—with no apparent source—are one telltale sign of a haunt. You may smell a spirit's favorite food, flower, perfume, or cologne. Ghosts can cause unpleasant scents, too—hot tar or cigar smoke, for instance. Please remember that nasty smells do not necessarily indicate that the *ghost* is nasty. The scent is simply a trademark for the deceased person. Maybe your ghost was a street engineer, or a cigar smoker.

The aroma in a room may represent some notable event in the ghost's earthly life. Let's suppose that you recently cleaned the cellar, but it suddenly begins smelling very damp and musty. The smell could be a sign that a flood occurred here, some time in the past. A ghost may have lived through that flood or died in it.

*Skeptical Advisor:* The smell could also be a scented energy imprint, rather than the work of a ghost. When you investigate any strange aroma, check within and around the area to determine if it has a natural cause. Look around, determine which way the wind is blowing, and find out what types of buildings and plants are nearby. Check the pets and children for possible influences. Such detailed measures are important in all your ghost hunting!

## Children and Pets

Children and animals are more sensitive to the presence of spirits than adults are. We need to pay more attention to their instincts, especially when we investigate hauntings. The following story is a case in point.

> I was moving some furniture around in my house, bringing an antique pedal sewing machine down from the attic. I stopped and left the machine on the landing to take a breather: at this point, my Keeshond started to bark wildly. He sat at the bottom of the stairs, looking intently at the machine, and would not stop barking until I moved it off the landing into the living room. Even then, the dog walked cautiously around the machine. It took a week for this behavior to wane. I believe this reaction was caused by a spirit attached to the machine, although I was oblivious to its presence.

The ancients regarded dogs as having a special gift—dogs could sense spirits. Certain animals—birds, for instance—may actually carry a spirit with them. Babies have free access to the spirit realms for a period just after they are born, because their crown chakra—located at the top of the head, where an infant has a "soft spot"—is open. Children are also more sensitive than adults, because children do not have as many conditioned responses to hinder or prejudice their perceptions.

So, if a child talks of a friend you can't see, get a description and listen closely to your child. If your pets take notice of something, and you see nothing, get ready: you may find yourself playing with that "nothing," or running from it, should it turn out to be a ghost.

*Skeptical Advisor:* Animals have a different range of hearing, smell, and vision than we do: they could be reacting to environmental causes, rather than ghosts. Children have rich imaginations, which are easily influenced by books and other media.

## Disappearing, Reappearing, or Rearranged Items

My roommate and I used to live with a spirit who delighted in straightening pictures and messing closets. The spirit would get busier whenever there was a lot of human activity in the house—numerous guests coming and going, or intense spring cleaning sessions. I have received descriptions of similar hauntings, in which books or jewelry disappear, only to reappear in unexpected places.

Try to determine why a spirit wants to rearrange or remove items. Taking jewelry or a book may be a way for it to feel closer to this world. A ghost who frequently throws cards around may have a moral taboo against card playing.

*Skeptical Advisor:* Did you move the suspect item yourself? You may not have been conscious of doing so. A playful pet or fairy may have moved it. In regions prone to tremors, objects are more likely to be displaced. Check whether the area is prone to drafts, or gusts of wind—especially if you are trying to account for lightweight items like playing cards.

## Dreams

Dreaming is honored and given great importance in many cultures. For Australian Aborigines, dreaming is the time when the living can commune with spirits, the ancestors, and the gods. In cultures as distant as Greece, Japan, and Germany, dreaming was regarded as a way to release the mind from its usual constraints, and to open it to new potential, including an awareness of a haunting.

The Greeks called the god of dreams Morpheus: he was the son of Hypnos ("Sleep") and a cousin to Thanatos

("Death"). Sleep and dream were states that had a unique connection to the afterlife and to the spirits that dwelt there. The connection was so strong that the Greeks believed that the people closest to death were also the best and most dependable dream oracles!

In ancient Japan, the Emperor was the official dreamer for his people. He would go into seclusion to commune with the supernatural world through his dreams. Upon waking, he would communicate these messages to his staff and the community.

In Germanic regions, people once believed that spirits who visited during sleep brought them luck and protection. Usually these spirits were female; they may have been a communal expression of the fertility goddess, or fate, in that culture.

The idea that sleepers could receive communications from spirits of the dead continued through the Renaissance. In the sixteenth century, the Swiss mystic and physician Paracelsus wrote that dreaming of people who had been dead for more than fifty years was one way to receive knowledge from the next world.

Poets as well as historians have recognized the connection between sleep, death, and dreams. Shakespeare's Hamlet concluded that suicide would not extinguish his consciousness, "for in that sleep of death what dreams may come." As early as 720 B.C., the Greek historian Hesiod spoke of sleep as the brother of death.

Sleep, death, and dreams are connected within the human consciousness; our dream time, then, can become like an inter-dimensional modem that intercepts and interprets messages from dimensions other than the waking world. While we sleep, our mind is less busy with mundane thoughts, so there is time and opportunity to access normally untapped portions of gray matter. We use about 30 percent of our brain's total capacity daily: what happens when someone opens the doorway to even five percent more? I believe that people who access these unexercised portions of their brains are those who have psychic abilities. Dream apparitions usually deal with someone very close to the dreamer. A ghost haunting a residence may try this avenue of communication, if it has a story to tell, or an unresolved issue. Such ghosts may look for any available, open-minded person. If you begin having dream encounters with a ghost, make detailed notes of anything it tells you, and of any recurrent scenarios. After a while, patterns should develop within your data. You can then check these against historical records, to determine what the ghost is trying to describe.

*Skeptical Advisor:* Our mind has a vast capacity to store information. During sleep, subconscious knowledge—such as regional history—can become available to us. Dreams are largely subjective: their content cannot be authenticated by anyone other than the dreamer. . . .

## Mood and Ambiance

The ambiance of a region or house is strongly associated with energy impressions and cumulative energy. If this ambiance is extremely specific and potent, you may have a ghost present. Have you ever walked into an unfamiliar place and felt totally uncomfortable with it? Your feeling may be due to the presence of an unhappy spirit, or to negative energy imprints.

*Skeptical Advisor:* Feelings of comfort and discomfort are subjective: they may simply be due to your level of self-confidence. Your impressions of a place can be subconsciously shaped by any information you heard about it, prior to visiting. If you were told the place was haunted, you will go into it expecting a spooky feeling.

## Noises

Footsteps, cupboards opening, windows closing, objects dragging—these noises are often reported as part of a haunting. A ghost may be attempting to tell a story with these noises. If the ghost always sat in a favorite rocking chair, for example, the sound of creaking floorboards might occur. If the ghost paced the floor waiting for errant children, footsteps might be heard. Knowing that ghosts use noises to communicate, Victorian sensitives often brought drums or tambourines to their séances. The instrument was set on a table so that the ghost's vibrations could set it off. Unfortunately, wiggling an elbow at an apt moment could imitate this effect.

In 1959, the Swedish film producer Friedrich Jurgenson captured the voices of the dead on a tape recorder. Interested in his results, a group of engineers and independent scientists attempted regulated experiments in the 1970s: these yielded numerous taped voices in a variety of languages. These became known as electronic voice phenomena (EVP). Other investigations ensued, some of which seemed to prove or disprove EVP.

*Skeptical Advisor:* If you hear odd noises, check for pets, children, mice, wind-sensitive items, loose boards, or rattling shutters, before you reach for your ghost-banishing guide. Even music boxes can sound suddenly, if a spring loosens over time.

## Physical Manifestations

Physical manifestations—incidents when a living person is brushed against by a ghost, or feels its touch—are rare. Touch is an intimate sense. Unless you are very open and sensitive to the spirit realm, you are unlikely to experience this. A ghost would have to exert tremendous energy in order to cause physical sensations in a living person.

*On the day after the anniversary of my father's death, my son came running downstairs, crying and visibly shaken. When asked what was wrong, he said that he woke to find grandpa in bed with him, but thought it was Santa Claus! After drying his tears and allaying his fears, I went to a private spot and had a heart-to-heart with my dad, explaining the inappropriateness of physical manifestations to children. Somehow the message got through. From that point forward he only appeared in my son's dreams.*

*Skeptical Advisor:* Muscle twitches, nerves firing, and even a light breeze can mimic a ghostly physical manifestation. Shiatsu practitioners and other touch therapists believe that our body remembers everything that happens to us, and that physical touch can release those memories. A touch in the right place may free up a buried memory; that memory may in turn be mistaken for a ghostly experience.

## Temperature Changes

The temperature of a haunted area may shift up or down, but experience teaches that it is most likely to drop down. We tend to associate coldness with the absence of life, so the effect may be partly psychological. We tend to "translate" an encounter with lifeless energy into a feeling of physical coldness. Hot spots, by the way, seem to happen where there has been a fire in the past, or where there is a very angry spirit.

*Skeptical Advisor:* Check for open windows, fans, refrigerators, and weather conditions that could cause the change in temperature. Ley lines, which are manifestations of the earth's aura, can cause false hot spots of a less dramatic nature. Increased energy along a ley line warms up the area. Hot spots can also be mimicked by a heating system with odd cracks in the ducts and similar mechanical objects.

The stereotypical ghost is wispy and shadowy, but in fact many ghosts are so solid that we mistake them for people. Most of us do not realize that we saw a ghost until it has faded away or walked through a wall! Most of us catch glimpses at random, and it is difficult to explain why or how. If our subconscious has a way to detect the presence of stranded souls and other spirits, it could then interpret them visually. It is a mysterious ability: psychics and clairvoyant mediums do have a knack for seeing ghosts, but may not be able to explain the mechanics of how they do it.

The camera can sometimes capture a visual manifestation. I have found startling images in snapshots I took in Scotland: one of a silvery-blue helmet on a bench in front of a castle; and another of pink and purple light in the shape of a woman's figure, standing near the headstone at Callanish. I had no intentions of capturing "ghosts" when I took these pictures, and they came from different rolls of film.

*Skeptical Advisor:* Floaters, odd light reflections, after-images caused by bright light or constant color stimulus, and unexpected memories all cause visual images that might be mistaken for ghosts. Review the environment for possible causes, and check your eyeglasses for smudges. A fogged lens, a random insect flying through the picture, double exposures, reflections, and technical problems can all cause imposters on developed film. . . .

## Remedying a Haunted Home or Object

If—after all your examination, deductive reasoning, and protective measures—you conclude that a ghost is present, you must decide what to do about it. One strategy is to do nothing at all. If the ghost isn't troublesome, you can decide to leave well enough alone and share the space peacefully. Many people, including fantasy author Katherine Kurtz, find it quite easy and enjoyable to live with their ghosts. This does mean that you must sometimes accommodate a spirit's preferences—leaving an object where the ghost likes it to stay, for instance. But that is the consideration you would naturally show to any resident of your home. Respect your specter's space, and it will often return the favor.

Hauntings that interrupt your sleep or personal life, or that scare children, call for action. Try simple and subtle banishings first before calling on a minister or resorting to more drastic measures. For example, your first approach could be to paint and thoroughly clean the affected area or object. While you do so, bless it in some manner appropriate to your faith. Do this as part of your weekly routine.

You may also consider burning cleansing herbs—such as sage, cedar, pine, and frankincense. These aromatics are associated with rites for the dead, and many psychics include them in purgative procedures. Local cooperatives or New Age stores stock aromatics like these, in oil form. Dab the oil on your doorways and windows to mark your personal space—but first make sure that you're not allergic to the scent.

When banishing a spirit, always move counterclockwise around the affected area or object. When blessing the space, move clockwise. You may also add inspirational music, or any other personal touches you find meaningful. . . .

These banishing measures probably won't eliminate energy imprints, unresolved issue ghosts, or spirits who simply don't care that they're dead. In such cases, you may wish to enlist the aid of an expert, or try to communicate directly with the spirit if no help is available. One word of caution: I recommend you find experienced help, even if it takes you a while. Not all spirits are nice, nor do all of them wish to move on to another residence or existence. This makes amateur ghost-banishing a risky endeavor, best handled with caution.

# Borley Rectory Was the Most Haunted House in England

Harry Price

By most accounts, Borley Rectory in County Essex, England, was a large, unattractive brick house built in 1863 by Henry Bull, a minister. Bull's family inhabited the house for about sixty years. After Bull's death, his son Harry took over the home and the rectorship. For a short time after the younger Bull's death there was no rector (minister) for the parish, and the house was empty. Supposedly, local people avoided the building, believing it was haunted. In 1928 G.E. Smith (also a minister) and his wife moved into the home, but left it within a year. During their stay there, a prominent news-paper, the London *Daily Mail*, published an article detailing supposed hauntings at the rectory. The article described a phantom nun and a phantom four-horse coach. According to local legends, the rectory had been built on the site of a medieval monastery where a tragic romance had occurred.

Harry Price, an investigator of the paranormal and the

Harry Price, *Confessions of a Ghost Hunter*. London: Putnam, 1936.

founder of the National Laboratory of Psychical Research in London, read the *Daily Mail* article. Intrigued, he visited the rectory and interviewed the Smiths and their servants. While Price was at the rectory, he, too, experienced some ghostly phenomena. The following viewpoint is taken from Price's book *Confessions of a Ghost Hunter.* Price describes the period in which the Smiths lived at Borley Rectory and his investigation thus far.

*Editor's Note: At the time Price wrote this article, he was keeping the location of this investigation confidential, so he changed the names of people and places or used an initial followed by a long dash, a common practice at the time. K——Manor is really Borley Rectory; the Percival family is really the Bull family; and Mr. Robinson and his wife are really the Smiths.*

On Tuesday, June 11, 1929, I was lunching with a friend, when his telephone bell rang. The call was for me, from the editor of a great London daily [newspaper]. He had been trying to find me all the morning. He told me an extraordinary story. It appeared that one of his representatives had sent in a report of a most unusual *Poltergeist* case that was disturbing the inmates of a country house somewhere in the Home Counties. He sought my co-operation in unravelling the mystery. His man had been at the house for two days and was impressed by what he had seen and heard. Would I take up the case? I eagerly accepted his invitation.

That same afternoon I telegraphed to the tenant saying I would be with him the next day. His reply was: 'Thank God—come quickly. Will expect you to lunch.' The next morning found my secretary and me speeding through the countryside full of hope as to what we were going to see. As we took turns at the wheel, we discussed what the trouble might be. My experience told me to look for a mischievous adolescent, rats, practical jokers—or the village idiot. I have wasted very many weeks in acquiring this knowledge. But, I argued, a London reporter is not easily impressed; usually he is hard-headed, sceptical, and prone to scoff at such things as 'ghosts'. If the representative of the *Daily*——was convinced of something abnormal, obviously the affair was worth inquiring into. We had been so busily discussing the case that, before we realised it, we discovered we were on the outskirts of W——, a market town. With considerable difficulty, we found our way to K—— Manor, which is situated in a tiny hamlet, seven miles off the main road, and near nowhere in particular. We found that the large entrance gates had been opened for us and, as I swung my car up the drive, we could see our host, Mr. H. Robinson,[1] and his wife waiting to welcome us. We jumped out and crossed the threshold of what I am certain is the most haunted house in England; a house in which I have seen and heard the most convincing, *Poltegeist* phenomena; and a house which, if it were in the market, I would purchase in order to study *in situ* manifestations of an absolutely abnormal nature. Not only as K—— Manor the perfect conception of a haunted house (as regards both situation and variety of phenomena), but its psychic history goes back many years and is fully documented.

At lunch we heard the complete history of the house and its traditions, together with a detailed account of those manifestations which had brought us to such an out-of-the-way spot. The account which follows is from the verbatim notes which my secretary made during lunch.

---

1. For obvious reasons, some of the names in this report are fictitious.

## The Most Haunted House in England

K—— Manor is a large house with nine acres of ground, through which runs a little stream that empties itself in a pond. The grounds are well wooded, and one path, known as the 'Nun's Walk', leads to the little church and church-yard. Contiguous to the walk on one side is a lawn. The house is not an old one, having been built about 1863. It was erected on the site of a twelfth-century monastery, the crypt of which is still preserved. For many years the property has belonged to the Percival family. The mansion was built by Mr. Thomas Percival, who resided there. He died there in 1897. His son, Mr. Walter Percival, then became the occupier. He succumbed to a painful and lingering illness in 1927. He died in the 'Blue Room'. A succession of owners occupied the mansion, but it was alleged that none would stop more than a few months, owing to the disturbances. In the spring of 1929 Mr. H. Robinson rented the house, and spent £200 on doing the place up; his occupation was the signal for a display of supernormal happenings which, eventually, drove him out. But I am anticipating.

Now for the traditions, because K—— Manor has several. At the period when the monastery was in its heyday, a coachman belonging to the establishment fell in love with a nun attached to a convent nearby. Their clandestine meetings culminated in an attempted elopement in a black coach drawn by two bay horses, driven by a lay brother. The trio were missed, overtaken, and brought back. The three were tried by their respective superiors. The maiden was walled up alive and the coachmen beheaded. So much for the principal legend—which has several variants. A more modern story tells how the apparition of Mr. Walter Percival is frequently seen, dressed in the old grey bed-jacket in which he died.

It is not clear whether the traditions have been built up on what a number of people undoubtedly think they have seen, or whether the 'appearances' are really the apparitions of the unfortunate mediaeval lovers and the late owner. But there is no doubt whatever that many people claim to have seen a coach and pair careering through the grounds of K——Manor, and, much more frequently, the figure of a nun slowly walking past the lawn towards the churchyard; that is how the 'Nun's Walk' got its name. But the nun and her male friends play only a very small part in the amazing story of K——.

## Troubling Incidents

By the time we had finished our coffee, I had heard the history of K—— and its ghostly inhabitants. But what interested me most was Mr. Robinson's story of his own experiences. Of course he heard all about the K—— legend before he took the place, but did not believe a word of it; he regarded as fantastic the stories that previous owners had departed on account of a 'ghost'. His incredulity rapidly gave place to something akin to fear.

The first 'incident' was the ringing of the front-door bell—a big, sonorous, clanging bell that reverberated all over the house. It was soon after the Robinsons moved in and they were just retiring to rest. It was a terrible night. There was a storm raging and it would be difficult to imagine a worse evening for anyone to be abroad. Mr. Robinson looked at his wife in wonderment. Thinking it was a neighbour in dire trouble, he hurried to the door and withdrew the bolts. The bell stopped ringing. With the lamp in one hand, he peered into the darkness: there was no one there. Sheltering the lamp from the gusts of wind and rain that threatened to extinguish it, he walked a few paces down the drive in search of his visitor. Nothing was to be seen. He went into the roadway, but not a soul was visible. He returned to the house and went to bed. Twenty-five minutes later (at about 11.45) the bell rang out again: not an ordinary ring, but a clangorous solo which lasted until he could get a dressing-gown on and reach the door. No one was there. The rain had then ceased, and thinking the intruder was a small boy playing a joke, he explored a considerable part of the garden and roadway: he found no one. There was no further disturbance that night, but the nocturnal clangour of the door bell rang in an orgy of ringing which persists to this day.

The bells were the start of the trouble. Only a part of the house was furnished, but bell-ropes in empty rooms were pulled as frequently as those in the apartments in use. And then the door-keys commenced to fall out of the locks. Every key would be in its place overnight; in the morning, many of them would be found on the floor. Eventually, *every one disappeared.*

With the key phenomena came the sounds of slippered footfalls, in all parts of the house, by day and by night. Especially when they were undressing for bed, the Robinsons would hear soft steps in the passage outside their room. More than once Mr. Robinson waited in the dark with a hockey stick and made lunges at 'something' that passed him. He never struck anything. Then stones were thrown: small round pebbles (origin unknown) were hurtled through the air, or came rolling down the stairs. Things became so bad that the villagers were frightened. A reporter arrived on the scene—and that is how I came to be connected with the case.

## A New Phenomenon

The night previous to my arrival, a new phenomenon was witnessed. It was reported by several people that a light had been seen at the window of one of the empty and disused rooms. It did not remain stationary, but appeared to travel in an elliptical path which was always visible from the garden. The reporter, who had by then established himself in the village, saw the light plainly and suggested to Mr. Robinson that the latter should go to the room with another light and explore. This was done and, for the space of about a minute, the watchers from the garden saw *two* lights side by side, one (our host's) being waved about, the other quite stationary. But Mr. Robinson neither saw nor heard anything in the room.

That was the latest story that was current when I arrived at the Manor on June 12. Having finished lunch, I asked to see the staff of the house. It consisted of a young village girl (who slept at home) and a daily gardener. Of course the girl knew all about the traditions of the place and solemnly assured me that she had seen 'an old-fashioned coach' on the lawn, 'drawn by two horses'. She said she had also seen the 'nun' leaning over a gate near the house. I then learnt that when the Robinsons moved in they brought with them from London a young maid who stayed for exactly forty-eight hours. Questioned about her sudden departure, she declared that near some trees in the garden she had seen a 'nun who had frightened her'. She had *not* been told about the tradition, but nothing would induce her to stop. I interviewed the old gardener, who informed me he had never seen the apparitions but had that very week dug up a skull (supposed to be a relic of the Great Plague) when removing some turf, and re-buried it in the churchyard.

I spent the remainder of the afternoon and early evening exploring every inch of the house, gardens, cellar, crypt, outhouses and stables (over which were some disused rooms). My secretary and I, in our minute examination of every bell wire, which we traced from the pull to the bell itself (they were the old-fashioned variety, on springs), climbed under the eaves and wormed our way between the top rafters and the tiles. We found a plaque on which the original bell-hangers had written their names, ages, and date, but discovered nothing else. Every wire seemed quite ordinary. We could find nothing suspicious in the house or grounds, so, after a meal, we settled down to wait for dusk.

## An Apparition

It is at dusk that the 'nun' is supposed to be most active, so the Pressman and I decided to spend the evening in the garden. My secretary was to report what took place in the house, where she was on guard. We arranged that I should keep my eyes glued on the back windows of the building in wait for the 'light', while the reporter watched the 'Nun's Walk'. As it was getting chilly, we stood in the doorway of a large summerhouse. We had been there nearly an hour when the reporter suddenly gripped my arm and whispered: 'There she is!' I looked towards the 'Nun's Walk' and sure enough there appeared to be a shadowy figure gliding down the path under the trees. As he spoke, the newspaper man dashed across the lawn. When he returned, he informed me that the figure became more distinct as he approached it, but vanished as he reached the spot. He told me that it just 'melted away'. I did not see this disappearance, as the reporter was between the figure and me. Concluding that the 'nun' would not be seen again that night, we decided to enter the house. As we passed under the porch, there was a terrific crash and a pane of glass from the roof hurtled to the ground.

The glass missed us by a few feet. It *may* have been coincidence that a pane of glass fell (for no ascertainable reason) just as we entered the porch, but it was very disconcerting. But that was not the worst. We entered the house and searched the place from roof to cellar. Just as we were coming downstairs after the investigation, a red glass candlestick, from the 'Blue Room', was flung down the staircase well and struck an iron stove in the hall. I was splashed with splinters. Immediately after, a mothball came tumbling down the well. The only persons in the house were *downstairs*. (The maid had gone home.)

## A Séance

I then decided to seal every door and window in the house. I fetched from my car the fitted case[2] which I carry on these occasions, and inserted screw-eyes in doors, posts, and window frames. Tapes were threaded through the eyes, knotted, and the knots sealed with post-office leaden seals. Then we adjourned to the 'Blue Room' to see what would happen. It was suggested by Mr. Robinson that we should hold a *séance* in this room, where Mr. Walter Percival had died. I was rather averse to the proposal, as we were not there to encourage the alleged 'spirits', but rather to disperse them. However, I gave way, but insisted upon the *séance* being held by the light of the powerful duplex paraffin lamp which we had carried upstairs. We seated ourselves on the bed and on the two chairs which the room contained, and I made a short speech, addressing my remarks to the four walls of the room. I protested that the manifestations were undermining the health of our host and his wife, and implored the disturbing entities, whether evil or benevolent, to depart. I then asked: 'Is Mr. Walter Percival present?' To our amazement,

---

2. The reader may be interested to know what a ghost-hunter's kit consists of. My bag contained: pair of soft felt overshoes, steel measuring tape; screw-eyes, lead seals and sealing tool; white tape; tool-pad and nails; hank of flex, small electric bells, dry batteries and switches (for secret electrical contacts); camera, films and flash-bulbs; note-book, red, blue and black pencils; sketching block and case of drawing instruments; bandages, iodine and surgical adhesive tape; ball of string, stick of chalk, matches, electric torch and candle; flask of brandy; bowl of mercury to detect tremors in room or passage; cinematograph camera with electrical release. For a long stay in house with supply of electricity, I would take with me infra-red filters, lamps, and ciné films sensitive to infra-red rays, so that I could photograph objects in almost complete darkness.

we were answered by a decided rap which appeared to come from the back of a large mirror which stood on the dressing table. It was then about one o'clock in the morning.

For three hours we questioned whatever it was that was rapping out answers. Once for 'yes', twice for 'no' and three times for 'doubtful' was the code which we suggested and which, apparently, the entity understood perfectly. We asked innumerable questions, which were prompted by a member of the Percival family, who was present. 'Walter Percival' discussed his will, his marriage and his relatives; and the answers we received—*via* the mirror—were always intelligent and relevant. We were informed that quite a number of 'family secrets' had been revealed.

Just before we closed this novel and extraordinary *séance*, a cake of soap in the washstand was lifted and thrown heavily on to a china jug which was standing on the floor with such force that the soap was deeply marked. All of us were on the other side of the room when this happened. We dispersed soon after, and I snatched a few hours' sleep on the bed in the 'Blue Room'. I was not disturbed: haunted and haunters were at peace.

Next morning I went into the town of W—— and interviewed the owners of K—— Manor. They were three sisters, two of whom I saw. They assured me that in 1900, during a garden party, on a sunny afternoon, the three sisters and a maid saw a nun, dressed completely in black, and with bowed head, slowly walking down the path. One of them said, 'I'll speak to her!' and ran across the lawn. As she approached, the figure turned its head and vanished. This story was confirmed by the other sister. The Misses Percival also informed me that their brother, Mr. Walter Percival, frequently saw the coach and nun. This was confirmed by a friend of the late owner who wrote to the *Daily*—— and stated that on several occasions Mr. Percival had admitted to him that he had seen both nun and coach; and that, when dead, he would, if possible, manifest in the same way. Did he partly fulfil this promise early that same morning when we were assembled in the 'Blue Room'?

## More Evidence

I received other evidence as to the haunting of K—— Manor. While I was in W—— I called on a man who was once groom-gardener at the house and who had lived in the rooms over the stables. Every night for eight months he and his wife, when in bed, heard steps in the living-room adjoining. The noises were as if a huge dog had jumped from some considerable height and had then started running round the room. One night there was heard a terrific crash as if the sideboard had toppled over, smashing the ornaments in its fall. The groom jumped out of bed, lit a candle, and went to explore. Not a thing was displaced—and the 'dog' was heard no more. During my investigation I received a letter from another old servant who, forty-three years previously, was an under-nursemaid at the Manor. She told me that it was common talk that the place was haunted. When she had been there a fortnight, she was awakened in the dead of night by someone moving outside her bedroom door. It sounded as if a person were shuffling about in slippers. The experience so unnerved her that her father removed her from the place. There is much good evidence for the haunting of K—— Manor.

# A Psychic's Visit Proves That San Diego's Whaley House Is Haunted

Hans Holzer

There is a two-story brick mansion in the Old Town section of San Diego, California, that was built in 1856 by Thomas Whaley. Whaley also built an annex to the house, which he rented to the county in 1869 to be used as the courthouse.

As San Diego grew, a strong rivalry developed between the Old Towners and the New Towners, who wanted the courthouse to be located in the new area of the town. In 1871, while Whaley was away, "a gang of New Towners broke into his house, terrorized his wife and daughter, and stole all the [court] records," reports Dennis William Hauck in his book *The National Directory of Haunted Places*. The gang also damaged the house, and Whaley was involved in a bitter twenty-year fight for reparations. Members of the

Hans Holzer, *Ghosts, Hauntings, and Possessions: The Best of Hans Holzer, Book I*. St. Paul, MN: Llewellyn Publications, 1991. Copyright © 1990 by Llewellyn Publications, Ltd. PO Box 64383, St. Paul, MN 55164. All rights reserved. Reproduced by permission.

Whaley family lived in the house until 1953, after which it fell into disrepair and was slated to be torn down.

In 1956 the Historical Shrine Foundation of San Diego County, an organization interested in the preservation of historic places, bought the home and restored it. Long reputed to be haunted, the Whaley House today is operated as a museum and tourist attraction. Many staff members and visitors have reported ghostly phenomena in the house, including several different apparitions, smells of cigar smoke and perfume, doors and windows opening and closing when no one is around, and many other strange occurrences.

In 1965 television talk-show host Regis Philbin invited Hans Holzer, a well-known ghost hunter, to conduct an investigation of the Whaley House for Philbin's television program. When Holzer investigates haunted places, he typically works with a trusted psychic whom he believes can sense and even communicate with ghosts. In the Whaley House investigation, he worked with Sybil Leek, a famous psychic and witch from England.

The following account focuses on Leek's trance-state communication with spirits in the house. It also includes a follow-up discussion Holzer held with June Reading, the Whaley House director, which confirmed many of the things Leek said during and after her trance and proved to Holzer that, indeed, Whaley House is haunted, Holzer, his wife Catherine, Philbin, June Reading, and James Reading (head of the organization responsible for the house) were all present during the investigation. Holzer has written many books and articles on ghosts and other paranormal topics, including *America's Ghosts*, *Ghosts: True Encounters with the World Beyond*, and *Real Hauntings: True American Ghost Stories*.

I started to look for [Sybil Leek] and found to my amazement that she had seated herself in one of the old chairs in what used to be the kitchen, downstairs in back of the living room. When I entered the room she seemed deep in thought, although not in trance by any means, and yet it took me a while to make her realize where we were.

Had anything unusual transpired while I was in the Court Room interviewing [witnesses]?

"I was standing in the entrance hall, looking at the postcards," Sybil recollected, "when I felt I just had to go to the kitchen, but I didn't go there at first, but went halfway up the stairs, and a child came down the stairs and into the kitchen and I followed her."

"A child?" I asked. I was quite sure there were no children among our party.

"I thought it was Regis' little girl and the next thing I recall I was in the rocking chair and you were saying something to me."

Needless to say, Regis Philbin's daughter had *not* been on the stairs. I asked for a detailed description of the child.

"It was a long-haired girl," Sybil said. "She was very quick, you know, in a longish dress. She went to the table in this room and I went to the chair. That's all I remember."

I decided to continue to question Sybil about any psychic impressions she might now gather in the house.

"There is a great deal of confusion in this house," she began. "Some of it is associated with another room upstairs, which has been structurally altered. There are two centers of activity."

Sybil, of course, could not have known that the house consisted of two separate units [the home and the courtroom annex]. "Any ghosts in the house?"

"Several," Sybil assured me. "At least four!"

Had not William Richardson's group [Richardson was one of the people Holzer interviewed later] made contact with a little girl ghost who had claimed that she knew of four other ghosts in the house? The report of that seance did not reach me until September, several months after our visit, so Sybil could not possibly have "read our minds" about it, since our minds had no such knowledge at that time.

"This room where you found me sitting," Sybil continued, "I found myself drawn to it; the impressions are very strong here. Especially that child—she died young."

We went about the house now, seeking further contacts.

"I have a date now," Sybil suddenly said, "1872."

The Readings exchanged significant glances. It was just after the greatest bitterness of the struggle between Old Town and New Town, when the removal of the Court records from Whaley House by force occurred.

"There are two sides to the house," Sybil continued. "One side I like, but not the other."

## Trance in the Court Room

Rather than have Sybil use up her energies in clairvoyance, I felt it best to try for a trance in the Court Room itself. This was arranged for quickly, with candles taking the place of electric lights except for what light was necessary for the motion picture cameras in the rear of the large room.

Regis Philbin and I sat at Sybil's sides as she slumped forward in a chair that may well have held a merciless judge in bygone years.

But the first communicator was neither the little girl nor the man in the frock coat. A feeble, plaintive voice was suddenly heard from Sybil's lips, quite unlike her own, a voice evidently parched with thirst.

"Bad . . . fever . . . everybody had the fever . . ."

"What year is this?"

"Forty-six."

I suggested that the fever had passed, and generally calmed the personality who did not respond to my request for identification.

"Send me . . . some water . . ." Sybil was still in trance, but herself now. Immediately she complained about there being a lot of confusion.

"This isn't the room where we're needed . . . the child . . . she is the one."

"What is her name?"

"Anna . . . Bell . . . she died very suddenly with something, when she was thirteen . . . chest . . ."

"Are her parents here too?"

"They come . . . the lady comes."

"What is this house used for?"

"Trade . . . selling things, buying and selling."

"Is there anyone other than the child in this house?"

"Child is the main one, because she doesn't understand anything at all. But there is something more vicious. Child would not hurt anyone. There's someone else. A man. He knows something about this house . . . about thirty-two, unusual name, C . . . Calstrop . . . five feet ten, wearing a green coat, darkish, mustache and side whiskers, he goes up to the bedroom on the left. He has business here. His business is with things that come from the sea. But it is the papers that worry him."

"What papers?" I demanded.

"The papers . . . 1872. About the house. Dividing the house was wrong. Two owners, he says."

"What is the house being used for, now, in 1872?"

"To live in. Two places . . . I get confused for I go one place and then I have to go to another."

"Did this man you see die here?"

"He died here. Unhappy because of the place . . . about the

other place. Two buildings. Some people quarreled about the spot. He is laughing. He wants all this house for himself."

"Does he know he is dead?" I asked the question that often brings forth much resistance to my quest for facts from those who cannot conceive of their status as "ghosts."

Sybil listened for a moment.

"He does as he wants in this house because he is going to live here," she finally said. *"It's his house."*

"Why is he laughing?"

A laughing ghost, indeed!

"He laughs because of people coming here thinking it's *their* house! When he knows the truth."

"What is his name?" I asked again.

"Cal . . . Caltrop . . . very difficult as he does not speak very clearly . . . he writes and writes . . . he makes a noise . . . he says he will make even more noise unless you go away."

"Let him," I said, cheerfully hoping I could tape-record the ghost's outbursts. "Tell him he has passed over and the matter is no longer important," I told Sybil.

"He is upstairs."

I asked that he walk upstairs so we could all hear him. There was nobody upstairs at this moment—everybody was watching the proceedings in the Court Room downstairs.

We kept our breath, waiting for the manifestations, but our ghost wouldn't play the game. I continued with my questions.

"What does he want?"

"He is just walking around, he can do as he likes," Sybil said. "He does not like new things . . . he does not like any noise . . . except when he makes it."

"Who plays the organ in this house?"

"He says his mother plays."

"What is her name?"

"Ann Lassay . . . that's wrong, it's Lann—he speaks so

badly . . . Lannay . . . his throat is bad or something . . ."

I later was able to check on this unusual name. Anna Lannay was Thomas Whaley's wife!

At the moment, however, I was not aware of this fact and pressed on with my interrogation. How did the ghost die? How long ago?

"'89 . . . he does not want to speak; he only wants to roam around . . ."

Actually, Whaley died in 1890. Had the long interval confused his sense of time? So many ghosts cannot recall exact dates but will remember circumstances and emotional experiences well.

## The Ghost Is Whaley

"He worries about the house . . . he wants the whole house . . . for himself . . . he says he will leave them . . . papers . . . hide the papers . . . he wants the other papers about the house . . . they're four miles from here . . . several people have these papers and you'll have to get them back or he'll never settle . . . never . . . and if he doesn't get the whole house back, he will be much worse . . . and then, the police will come . . . he will make the lights come and the noise . . . and the bell . . . make the police come and see him, the master . . . of the house, he hears bells upstairs . . . he doesn't know what it is . . . he goes upstairs and opens the windows, wooden windows and looks out . . . and then he pulls the . . . no, it's not a bell . . . he'll do it again . . . when he wants someone to know that he really is the master of the house . . . people today come and say he is not, but he is!"

I was surprised. Sybil had no knowledge of the disturbances, the alarm bell, the footsteps, the open window . . . yet it was all perfectly true. Surely, her communicator was our man!

"When did he do this the last time?" I inquired.

"This year . . . not long . . ."

"Has he done anything else in this house?"

"He said he moved the lights. In the parlor."

Later I thought of the Richardson seance and the lights they had observed, but of course I had no idea of this when we were at the house ourselves.

"What about the front door?"

"If people come, he goes into the garden . . . walks around . . . because he meets mother there."

"What is in the kitchen?"

"Child goes to the kitchen. I have to leave him, and he doesn't want to be left . . . it was an injustice, anyway, don't like it . . . the child is twelve . . . chest trouble . . . something from the kitchen . . . bad affair . . ."

"Anyone's fault?"

"Yes. Not chest . . . from the cupboard, took something . . . it was an acid like salt, and she ate it . . . she did not know . . . there is something strange about this child, someone had control of her, you see, she was in the way . . . family . . . one girl . . . those boys were not too good . . . the other boys who came down . . . she is like two people . . . someone controlled her . . . made her do strange things and then . . . could she do that . . ."

"Was she the daughter of the man?"

"Strange man, he doesn't care so much about the girl as he does about the house. He is disturbed."

## More Ghosts

"Is there a woman in this house?"

"Of course. There is a woman in the garden."

"Who is she?"

"Mother. Grandmother of the girl."

"Is he aware of the fact he has no physical body?"

"No."

"Doesn't he see all the people who come here?"

"They have to be fought off, sent away."

"Tell him it is now seventy years later."

"He says seventy years when the house was built."

"Another seventy years have gone by," I insisted.

"Only part of you is in the house."

"No, part of the house . . . you're making the mistake," he replied.

I tried hard to convince him of the real circumstances. Finally, I assured him that the entire house was, in effect, his.

Would this help?

"He is vicious," Sybil explains. "He will have his revenge on the house."

I explained that his enemies were all dead.

"He says it was an injustice, and the Court was wrong and you have to tell everyone this is his house and land and home."

I promised to do so and intoned the usual formula for the release of earthbound people who have passed over and don't realize it. Then I recalled Sybil to her own self, and within a few moments she was indeed in full control.

## History and the Ghosts

I then turned to the director of the museum, Mrs. Reading, and asked for her comments on the truth of the material just heard.

"There was a litigation," she said. "The injustice could perhaps refer to the County's occupancy of this portion of the house from 1869 to 1871. Whaley's contract, which we have, shows that this portion of the house was leased to the County, and he was to supply the furniture and set it up as a Court Room. He also put in the two windows to provide light. It was a valid agreement. They adhered to the contract as long as the Court continued to function here, but when

Alonzo Horton came and developed New Town, a hot contest began between the two communities for the possession of the county seat. When the records were forcefully removed from here, Whaley felt it was quite an injustice, and we have letters he addressed to the Board of Supervisors, referring to the fact that his lease had been broken. The Clerk notified him that they were no longer responsible for the use of this house—after all the work he had put in to remodel it for their use. He would bring the matter up periodically with the Board of Supervisors, but it was tabled by them each time it came up."

"In other words, this is the injustice referred to by the ghost?"

"In 1872 he was bitterly engaged in asking redress from the County over this matter, which troubled him some since he did not believe a government official would act in this manner. It was never settled, however, and Whaley was left holding the bag."

"Was there a child in the room upstairs?"

"In the nursery? There were several children there. One child died here. But this was a boy."

Again, later, I saw that the Richardson seance spoke of a boy ghost in the house.

At the very beginning of trance, before I began taping the utterances from Sybil's lips, I took some handwritten notes. The personality, I now saw, who had died of a bad fever had given the faintly pronounced name of Fedor and spoke of a mill where he worked. Was there any sense to this?

"Yes," Mrs. Reading confirmed, "this room we are in now served as a granary at one time. About 1855 to 1867."

"Were there ever any Russians in this area?"

"There was a considerable otter trade here prior to the American occupation of the area. We have found evidence that the Russians established wells in this area. They came into these waters then to trade otters."

"Amazing," I conceded. How could Sybil, even if she wanted to, have known of such an obscure fact?

"This would have been in the 1800's," Mrs. Reading continued. "Before then there were Spaniards here, of course."

"Anything else you wish to comment upon in the trance session you have just witnessed?" I asked.

Mrs. Reading expressed what we all felt.

"The references to the windows opening upstairs, and the ringing of these bells . . ."

How could Sybil have known all that? Nobody told her and she had not had a chance to acquaint herself with the details of the disturbances.

## The "Other House" Explained

What remained were the puzzling statements about "the other house." They, too, were soon to be explained. We were walking through the garden now and inspected the rear portion of the Whaley house. In back of it, we discovered to our surprise still another wooden house standing in the garden. I questioned Mrs. Reading about this second house.

"The Pendington House, in order to save it, had to be moved out of the path of the freeway . . . it never belonged to the Whaleys although Thomas Whaley once tried to rent it. But it was always rented to someone else."

No wonder the ghost was angry about "the other house." It had been moved and put on *his* land without his consent!

The name *Cal . . . trop* still did not fall into place. It was too far removed from Whaley and yet everything else that had come through Sybil clearly fitted Thomas Whaley. Then the light began to dawn, thanks to Mrs. Reading's detailed knowledge of the house.

"It was interesting to hear Mrs. Leek say there was a store here once . . ." she explained. "This is correct, there was a store here at one time, but it was not Mr. Whaley's."

"Whose was it?"

"It belonged to a man named Wallack . . . Hal Wallack . . . that was in the seventies."

Close enough to Sybil's tentative pronunciation of a name she caught connected with the house.

"He rented it to Wallack for six months, then Wallack sold out," Mrs. Reading explained.

I also discovered, in discussing the case with Mrs. Reading, that the disturbances really began after the second house had been placed on the grounds. Was that the straw that broke the ghost's patience?

Later, we followed Sybil to a wall adjoining the garden, a wall, I should add, where there was no visible door. But Sybil insisted there had been a French window there, and indeed there was at one time. In a straight line from this spot, we wound up at a huge tree. It was here, Sybil explained, that Whaley and his mother often met—or are meeting, as the case may be.

I was not sure that Mr. Whaley had taken my advice to heart and moved out of what was, after all, his house. Why should he? The County had not seen fit to undo an old wrong.

We left the next morning, hoping that at the very least we had let the restless one know someone cared.

# The Amityville House Was Haunted by Demons

Ed Warren and Lorraine Warren with Robert David Chase

An ordinary-looking Dutch colonial house brought world-wide notoriety to Amityville, a suburban community on Long Island, New York, when a book called *The Amityville Horror* by Jay Anson hit the best-seller lists in 1977 and was followed up by a hit movie. The book and movie were based on events that supposedly took place in the house during the month George and Kathleen Lutz and Kathleen's three children lived there.

The Lutz family bought the house and moved in on December 18, 1975. They moved out on January 14, 1976, claiming they had been terrorized by demons. According to Rosemary Ellen Guiley in *The Encyclopedia of Ghosts and Spirits*, "Ghostly apparitions of hooded figures, clouds of flies in the sewing room and children's playroom, windowpanes that broke simultaneously, bone-chilling cold alternating with suffocating heat, personality changes [in the family members], nightly parades by spirit marching bands, levitations, green slime spilling down stairs, putrid smells, sickness, strange scratches on Kathleen's body, objects moving of their own accord, repeated disconnection of telephone service, and even communications between the youngest [child], Melissa (Missy), and a devilish spirit pig she called 'Jodie' turned their dream home into a hell on earth." What could have possibly caused these things—and did they really happen?

The house had a frightening recent history. In November 1974, twenty-three-year-old Ronnie DeFeo had slaughtered his father, mother, and four younger siblings there. According to some reports, he claimed that demons had urged him to do this. Was it possible that the house was haunted by demons?

Ed Warren and Lorraine Warren, famous demonologists, were among those who visited the home hoping to discover its secrets. The Warrens are known for going to haunted places, where Lorraine says she communicates psychically with the spirits there. In the following selection, author Robert David Chase interviews the Warrens about their experiences in the Amityville house. Since this interview was first published, most people have come to believe that the Amityville affair was a hoax. However, the Warrens stand by their claim that demons haunted the house.

The Warrens are the founders of the New England Society for Psychic Research and have written many books and articles about their demon-hunting experiences.

*Few cases of the supernatural are as misunderstood as the one involving the Lutz family in Amityville. Because there has been so much publicity surrounding the case, many myths have been offered as fact.*

*During the course of our lectures, our audiences inevitably bring up the subject, and we take the time and patience to set the record straight.*

*We think it's fine that the topic continues to generate interest—as long as the truth is told.*

*—Lorraine Warren*

Q: When we talk about the "Amityville horror" what, specifically, are we referring to?

Lorraine: Early in the morning of November 13, 1974, one of the sons of the DeFeo family took a high-powered rifle and killed the other six members of his family.

Q: That's the Amityville horror?

Lorraine: That and what followed when George and Kathleen Lutz moved in thirteen months after the murders occurred.

Q: The house had stood empty during that time?

Lorraine: Yes. Local people feared the house. Nobody wanted to buy it. There was a great deal of publicity surrounding the DeFeo murders, and the house acquired a grim reputation.

Q: Did some people feel that the DeFeo boy had been possessed when he'd killed his family?

Lorraine: Oh, yes, most definitely. As I said, there was a great deal of press about the tragedy, and invariably the stories started about demonic possession.

Q: The Lutzes didn't care about all this talk?

Lorraine: They didn't know about it. Not exactly, anyway. They were young and a good, strong family and I suppose the stories seemed silly to them.

Q: So they moved in?

Lorraine: Yes, they did, near Christmastime. Neither Ed nor I can testify firsthand to anything that happened in the Lutz house—we have to take Jay Anson's words for those events. He wrote the famous book about Amityville.

Q: The Lutzes had problems in the house?

Lorraine: Yes, and almost immediately.

Q: How would you characterize those problems?

## Personality Disintegration

Lorraine: Well, for one thing, both George and Kathleen experienced what psychologists call personality disintegration.

Ed: When you look through many of the cases we investigate, you see that during the course of demonic possession, a person begins to change. "Fred isn't himself anymore," we hear frequently. Or "Judy just doesn't normally do things like this." The loved ones of the possessed find it almost impossible to accept these behavioral changes. They can't imagine what could possibly change a person so profoundly.

Q: And you say this happened to the Lutzes?

Ed: George Lutz—again, all this is according to Jay Anson—went from a rock solid, hard-working man to a real slob given to volcanic shifts of temper.

Q: Was Kathleen Lutz affected?

Lorraine: Absolutely. Normally a very easygoing, pleasant person, she found herself turning angry for no reason she could see. It was as if something inside her were dictating her behavior.

Q: And things began happening in the house?

Lorraine: Jay Anson's theory seemed to be that whatever demonic spirit had troubled the DeFeo boy was still loose in the house.

Q: So Anson was definitely convinced that the Lutzes were dealing with demonic possession?

Ed: In some respects, there could be no other explanation for what Anson claimed had happened.

Q: You seem cautious about Jay Anson's interpretation of the case.

Ed: My sense is that some things got dramatized beyond reality.

Q: Does this discredit the case?

Ed: Not at all.

Q: Then you think the Amityville horror took place as Anson suggested.

Ed: By and large. At least, his version of demonic infestation certainly squares with ours.

Q: In what way?

Ed: Well, look at the things the Lutzes reported. Hundreds of huge black flies appeared in the upstairs bedroom. The inside of the toilet bowls turned black, as if someone had painted them. A large statue moved around the house of its own volition. Windows opened and closed for no apparent reason.

Lorraine: Plus both George and Kathleen Lutz told of freezing temperatures that would not abate no matter how high they turned the heat—and then of sweltering heat that stayed with them no matter how many windows they opened.

Q: And you've experienced this with demonic infestation?

Ed: Oh, sure. Psychic cold, particularly.

Q: All this happened to the Lutzes over a short period of time, didn't it?

Ed: Yes; over a Christmas season.

Q: Then they moved?

Lorraine: Then they moved. Things had become pretty bad there.

Q: Worse than you've described so far?

Lorraine: Much worse. Kathleen was beginning to have dreams—nightmares, really—that involved the DeFeo family. They were quite vivid and quite disturbing.

Ed: Plus, the infestation itself had gotten worse.

Lorraine: A crucifix was turned upside down, for example, and that's almost always a sign that demons have begun to assert themselves.

Ed: And their children were beginning to be hurt. A boy got his hand crushed, though later there was no physical evidence of this. The demons were forcing family members to hallucinate, which, in some respects, can be the most frightening aspect of infestation.

Lorraine: And the Lutzes started to doubt their own sanity.

Ed: That's something we encounter very often.

Lorraine: We go into a house and interview the people and they tell us all sorts of things about what's been going on there—but rather than believe their own eyes and ears, they ask us if we think they're insane.

Ed: Most people in our society are trained to disbelieve in the demonic world.

Lorraine: Notice sometime how many laughs comedians get out of jokes about the demonic.

Ed: Most of us just don't want to deal with the demonic. Emotionally, we feel we can't. So we need to discredit it by saying that it's all imaginary.

Lorraine: It's easier for most people to think they're going insane than to deal with the possibility of demonic attack.

Ed: Psychologists call this denial, and we see this all the time. People just can't cope with the unknown.

Q: And that's what was going on with the Lutzes?

Ed: According to Anson, it was. And when you think about it, it's a natural reaction to stress. You don't want to admit what's really going on so you come up with a more comfortable explanation. "We've moved into a new house where something bad happened awhile back and we're just letting our imaginations run away with themselves." See? No real problem here. Nothing that good old reality can't handle.

Q: But they found out soon enough that "reality" couldn't explain what was going on?

Lorraine: Exactly.

Q: So where did that leave them?

Ed: Put yourself in their position. They're undergoing these radical transformations of personality—they've begun fighting with a viciousness that would have seemed impossible only a few weeks earlier—and all of a sudden doors are torn off their hinges and strange voices come from empty rooms and the children are deeply disturbed by it all.

Lorraine: So what do you do?

Ed: Ultimately they moved, of course, and that was the sensible thing to do.

Q: Did it work? Was that the last of their demonic infestation?

Ed: Apparently.

Q: You sound hesitant.

Ed: Well, moving isn't always a solution. We know families who've moved into infested houses and tried to move away—only to have the demons follow them.

Q: That must be horrifying.

Lorraine: We know families who've fought this kind of infestation for years.

Q: So what did the Lutzes conclude when they left?

Lorraine: The impression we got from Jay Anson was that they may have moved just in time.

Ed: What George, in particular, was concerned about was that some member of the family—and he certainly included himself as a possibility—would do what the DeFeo boy did: pick up a shotgun and kill everybody in the family.

Q: He felt that this was where the whole experience was leading?

Ed: Again, that's the impression we got.

Q: Do you think that was a real possibility?

Ed: Certainly.

Lorraine: Just because it happened once didn't mean it couldn't happen again. George Lutz was probably right to worry about that.

Q: So there could have been another tragedy?

Ed: Easily. As we saw in The Devil in Connecticut case, where a young man who was possessed murdered his employer, demonic infestation often inclines a person to violence. And the problem is, you're never sure which person in a family will be overcome by this urge.

Lorraine: In the case of the DeFeos, for example, it was the son. Why not the father or mother?

## Don't Wait

Q: So if people find themselves in a circumstance similar to Amityville—where they're finding themselves changing personalities in unmistakable ways and where strange events are beginning to take place—what should they do?

Ed: Talk to their pastor as soon as possible. And if their pastor won't help them, find knowledgeable demonologists to assist them.

Lorraine: They're free to contact us too.

Q: But don't wait, is that what you're saying?

Ed: If you have legitimate reason to think that you or any of your family has come under the powers of the demonic, then the worst thing you can do is wait.

Q: That was a serious offer—they can contact you?

Lorraine: Sure. People contact us all the time.

Q: You think the Lutzes acted promptly, then?

Ed: Given all that had happened to them in so short a time, yes.

Lorraine: As soon as they became convinced that there could be no other explanation for these events—they moved.

Q: Do books such as *The Exorcist* and *The Amityville Horror* help or hurt your cause?

Ed: The honest answer to that is "both." While they often overdramatize the demonic and risk having the public laugh instead of being curious enough to study the subject further, they do at least raise the topic in a sobering way.

Lorraine: *The Amityville Horror,* if nothing else, showed how a cursed house can affect very different families. And it showed how demonic infestation is a reality that can invade anyone's life.

Q: The Lutzes did seem like a pretty normal family.

Lorraine: Very normal. Very loving. And that's what made their experience all the more horrifying.

# Three Steps for Dealing with Ghosts

Peter Carter

What would you do if you thought your house was haunted by a ghost or poltergeist? In the following selection, Peter Carter tells the story of a woman who believed she had a haunted apartment. He also discusses the troublesome symptoms in other haunted homes. Carter describes his three-step plan for dealing with haunted abodes, including the use of a feng shui practitioner. Feng shui is the Chinese art of arranging one's environment so that it invites good spirits and repels bad ones.

Carter is a senior editor at *Chatelaine* magazine.

"Ourfatherwhoartinheavenhallowedbethynamethy—oh jeez what comes next?" Paula was choking on her own fear, and familiar words had escaped her for a moment. She was sitting in a dark room, praying at an auctioneer's pace because seconds earlier, she had stared down a ghost and told it to get out. Leave. Go back to where it came from. In doing so, she scared herself silly.

The ghost was in her friend Kate's apartment, and Kate—who felt too worn down by living with the ghost to actually confront it herself—had asked Paula to come over and evict it. "Just like Kate predicted, the thing arrived on schedule, at about 4 A.M.," Paula told me a few days afterward. "As soon as I said, 'You don't belong here, you have to leave now,' I started praying and never went so fast in my life."

Kate rents the first floor of a two-storey, 80-year-old brick house on a quiet narrow street in a working-class neighborhood about 20 minutes by foot west of downtown Toronto [Canada]. The houses are older, jammed together and have carefully tended gardens and front lawns barely larger than bath mats. Kate, single and in her early 40s, moved in two and a half years ago. She loves the area, dotes on her garden and thinks she couldn't find more suitable digs anywhere in the city. Like most people interviewed for this article, she didn't want her real name used; seems a haunting can leave you uneasy about publicity.

## The Incidents

The problems started the day she moved in. She was hanging some black-and-white prints in her new bedroom and standing on a chair. A force, not unlike a shove on shoulder, pushed her backward across the room and onto her backside. Kate, a practical entrepreneur . . . dismissed the event. "There was no reason to think about ghosts or anything, so I convinced myself that it was just an accident."

Over the next months, things worsened. She found herself waking up about 4 A.M. almost every night, feeling like someone had roused her. Once in a while—and a friend corroborated this—something could be heard pacing the floor at the end of her bed. "But mostly, it was a presence. I'd wake up and just feel that somebody's there. Sometimes, I'd go back to sleep, sometimes I'd just lie there frustrated." She never saw anything—just felt it.

It didn't happen every night, so she did her best to ignore it. But the pictures that she'd hung wouldn't stay put. Kate would come home to find them crooked or fallen to the floor. "I used to think that somebody had been snooping around." There were other signs: a friend borrowed the apartment for a weekend while Kate was out of town and the visitor's cat died, "for no apparent reason, in the middle of the night."

This past January [1998], she woke at 4 (again), felt the presence and, exasperated, dismissed it with an "Oh, go away." In the apartment above Kate lay Jennifer, an actor and musician. She too was in bed alone. And as the two women discovered the next morning, at the exact time that Kate shooed the ghost away, Jennifer felt something jostle her awake. "It was like somebody grabbed my foot and twisted it," she says. From then on, Jennifer agreed with Kate. Something was there.

By the time I met Kate, the late-night rousings had become commonplace. She hadn't had a good night's sleep in weeks. She had consulted a local priest about exorcising her ghost, and he told her she was imagining things. Now she was ready to give up. "It's not even that I'm scared so much as I'm tired and being sleepy all the time clouds my judgment," she told me. "Either the ghost goes," Kate sighed, "or I do."

## A Plan

I had a plan. Step 1: dispatch somebody to tell the ghost to get out. I had recently read about a New England woman whose visiting mother faced down a ghost that had been causing trouble. She told it, sternly, to go and it went. Why not try that at Kate's place? That's when Kate enlisted her gutsy pal Paula. If that wouldn't work, we would proceed to Step 2.

Paula did her thing—and by sunrise or so her heart rate had slowed down close to normal. The presence appeared again the following night. Kate said she had no choice but to go with Step 2.

## Disruptive Ghosts

Do ghosts really exist? Even if you don't exactly believe, it's hard to argue with writer John Robert Colombo, who cataloged more than 50 alleged hauntings, including the ghost of a blond-haired prisoner who revisits the city's infamous Don Jail, for his book *Haunted Toronto*. Colombo writes, "Ghosts belong to the category of experience, not to the category of belief."

Everybody knows somebody who insists that he or she lived in or stayed in or walked by a haunted house. In cities such as Halifax, St. John's and, intermittently, Victoria, you can actually go on ghost walks—tours of buildings and other sites reputed to be haunted. Some commercial establishments, especially bed-and-breakfast operations, actually boast of having ghosts. Eager patrons assume that if the ghosts actually exist, they're benign—that at worst, they'll rattle the pipes or play games with light.

But ghosts—or hauntings—are anything but amusing if they're disrupting your life.

Just ask Tara, a flight attendant who lives in Calgary with her husband, David, and their two preschool girls. They're in their second house now. Mysterious protuberances in the walls, discolored fixtures and inexplicable disappearances forced them out of their first.

The couple's honeymoon home was unique—a gabled two-storey 1912 farmhouse in a neighborhood of '50s bungalows. "Just by looking at the house, you could see that it stood out from the others on the block. As soon as we saw it, we fell in love with it."

First, mail went missing, for weeks at a time. "We asked the post office, they said it was delivered, but we never saw it. All kinds of things we should have been getting, letters, invoices."

Next, the poltergeist appeared. "We had friends over for the evening. We were standing around talking and somebody noticed the strangest thing—the middle of the living room wall started to bulge out, as if there was a huge balloon being blown up underneath the drywall."

The guests were dumbstruck. "Okay, maybe we'd all had a few drinks," Tara laughs, "but not that many." The bubble deflated in minutes but the paint remained scarred. "Another time," she says, "David was out of town and I went upstairs to the bathroom and all of the fixtures had changed color from white to a striped grey." The stripes were embedded, like marble, into the tub, the sink, everywhere. She investigated the discoloration, which appeared permanent, and no one could explain it. Tara hit a similar dead end when one day she found her toilet levered clear off its base so the water was running all over the floor, as if somebody lifted the commode with a crowbar. The plumber was mystified.

"Nobody could help us. We ended up so anxious that we bought another house before we even sold that one." When she talks about selling, Tara's tone becomes softer, a bit hesitant, because she knows that introducing a ghost into a real estate deal can be tricky. It didn't affect her, but she's lucky she doesn't live in a place like Nyack, N.Y., a community just north of Manhattan. A few years ago, a judge there ruled in favor of a home buyer who sued the sellers after he found out that his house was haunted and the previous owners knew it. Several states have laws where a home-owner who suspects her place is haunted is obliged to mention the fact to prospective buyers. And even a rumor of a haunting can hurt the price of a house.

## Fond Memories?

Four years have passed since Tara and David moved. The events that were so scary back then have been smoothed over with the laminate of time. It's common with stories of haunted houses. As the gap between the events and the telling grows wider, the frightening moments change into less threatening, almost fond memories.

But not that fond. My two sisters were forced out of an apartment that was haunted, and although it happened back in 1976, as soon as I begin to recall the episodes leading up to their departure, I get the same sensation I'd have if a cold-handed masseur gently kneaded the top disc of my backbone, then continued the pressure swiftly, ticklishly south until my spine tingled.

Norma and Bertholde had moved back to Sudbury, our hometown, from Toronto, and rented a two-bedroom apartment in a three-storey multiplex on a quiet street. Soon after they moved in, a souvenir plate that they'd hung on the kitchen flew across the room and smashed.

Other strange things happened in the bedroom where Norma slept. The drapes would blow as if the wind was catching them, even though the window was shut tight. And Norma would sometimes be awakened by banging noises, as if someone was clapping two planks together. Strangely, you couldn't hear them if you were standing but a few inches outside the bedroom door.

Friends and relatives slept over, simply because we found it hard to believe their stories. By the time of my visit,

Norma had vacated her bedroom and shared the remaining room with Bertholde. I went to bed in the haunted room. Just around 3 A.M., I jumped awake to a banging as loud as a baseball bat on a garbage can. "Don't worry, Peter," I heard a voice say, "It's only me." Assuming it was Norma, I went back to sleep, reassured.

The next day, Norma told me that neither she nor Bertholde had uttered a word.

Perplexed and a little scared by all the goings-on, Norma and Bertholde turned to Prof. Michael Persinger from Laurentian University. Persinger has made a name for himself as a professional skeptic who investigates and explains paranormal activities. He set up carefully calibrated seismographs and magnetic detectors throughout the apartment to see if he could detect any unusual electromagnetic events. Indeed, his machine did record mysterious movements in the haunted room. Here's how he described the events in a 1984 article in *The Journal of the American Society for Psychical Research:* "Two unusually intense electromagnetic events lasting for about 10 seconds each were recorded during 15 successive nightly eight-hour continuous measurements during the last stages of a possible poltergeist/haunt episode." Persinger attempts to link the hauntings to brief focused magnetic fields resulting from the shifting underground rock formations beneath Sudbury, a city built on top of mines. (One thing Persinger did not mention was the fact that Bertholde and Norma invited their priest to bless the apartment. He visited, prayed and immediately started getting sick. He left for home and reported the next day that the farther he drove from the apartment, the healthier he felt.)

Whether or not Persinger was right about shifting rock formations, his theories did nothing to make the apartment more hospitable. Norma, who had moved into the apartment in September, was out by Christmas. Bertholde stayed a few months longer but eventually, she too couldn't stay. The nightmare never let up.

## Step 2

That's why I appreciated the seriousness of Kate's plight. And it's the reason we agreed to proceed to Step 2 of our ghost-busting plan: we would turn to the ancient Chinese art of feng shui. We'd call Ivan Yip.

Yip graduated from the University of Toronto in 1962 and was a forensic scientist with the Ontario Attorney General's office until 1988. The next year, he began private practice as an architectural consultant, specializing in feng shui, the Chinese tradition of making sure that all the elements in a business or living space are arranged so they are in natural harmony with their surroundings. As exotic as it sounds, companies and thousands of private homeowners pay big money to have people like Yip give them advice. Yip himself has worked for clients from Hong Kong to Texas, including the Toronto-Dominion Bank, Cathay Pacific Airways and a housing development in Markham, Ontario.

I found him through a friend, a businessman who had hired Yip to "feng shui" his office. Yip says hauntings amount to 2 percent of his work, although he didn't want to tell me the names of any clients.

Yip is slender and shortish with large unblinking eyes. He wears a rumpled suit and when he talks he has a way of rocking toward you, as if he were beseeching you to listen—and believe. For the first hour of his visit to Kate's apartment, he proselytized, trying to get us to believe we were getting something worthwhile for our money ($100 each for Kate's and Jennifer's apartments).

He has no problem discussing ghosts as if they were as real as the person sitting next to you. "They are the spirits of dead people who didn't get promoted to the next dimension. Maybe they didn't lead good lives."

"Ghosts are like radio waves," he said, "and you can only detect them if your personal aerials are set to receive them." Adjust your personal antenna, and you won't pick up the signal anymore. "Ghost would still be there, but you couldn't see it or feel it." The way to reset your dial is to conduct a feng shui reading of the house and then change the orientation of whatever affects the energy. It actually sounded to me a lot like Persinger's explanations.

Yip rose from Kate's couch and took out his geomancy compass. The tool consists of a five-centimetre-in-diameter compass encircled by something that resembles a slide rule, flail of Chinese characters laid out in concentric circles. He took readings in nine different locations in each apartment. At each spot, he stood facing westward, held the compass in front of himself like a waiter proffering a tray, and measured his position relative to that of the compass needle. He added the measurements and divided by nine to find an average.

Based on his calculations, he divided the apartment into nine sections and told Kate and Jennifer which parts of the rooms were better for which activities, and how they can improve their general health and well-being by altering the decor or furnishings. For instance, he said, the southwest corner is the "prosperity corner"—a good place to conduct business and an ideal home for natural symbols of business, like gold and water. "A goldfish tank would go good there. Be very good for business."

But what about the ghosts? Yip entered Kate's bedroom, casually plunked himself on her bed with his stockinged feet toward the foot and his back against the headboard, and took some readings with his compass. "How d'you sleep when you see the ghost?" he asked Kate. "With feet pointing here?" She nodded.

"You should sleep like this," he said, angling himself diagonally across the mattress. "Or turn the bed on a new angle, just a little bit, like this."

"It's as simple as that?" Kate responded.

"Ghost should go," said Yip. Moments later, he was out the door. That night, Kate shifted her bed ever so slightly and slept soundly for the first time in months.

Did we have Kate's ghost licked? It's too early to know. A few weeks have passed since Yip's visit, and Kate has been away for most of that time. There have been no recurrences, but the hot weather may be a factor too; Kate acknowledges that the poltergeist had been much more bothersome in winter. Both Kate and Jennifer are rearranging their furniture and acting on Yip's feng shui advice, and they're keeping their fingers crossed.

## Step 3

But Kate and I are staying in touch. If the feng shui doesn't silence her poltergeist, I feel duty bound to help her with Step 3 of the plan. After all, I have a minivan, which comes in handy on moving day.

# A Modern Ghostbuster's Toolkit

Randolph W. Liebeck

The investigation of haunted houses started in earnest during the nineteenth century, when a strong spiritualism movement took place in Europe and North America. Spiritualists held that when people died, their spirits lived on and could contact or be contacted by the living. People could gain comfort or advice by communicating with their loved ones. However, spiritualism was rife with phonies—fraudulent mediums (people who supposedly contact the dead) and fake séances (meetings led by a medium during which spirits often were said to materialize or show themselves in some way, such as appearing, talking, or moving objects) abounded. Wishing to expose the frauds while at the same time prove that it truly was possible to communicate with the dead, the Society for Psychical Research (SPR) in England began to collect personal accounts of hauntings and investigated haunted houses and other places. The organization's methods, which remained in use until the late twentieth century, largely involved eliminating as many natural explanations as possible and using psychics to verify the presence of spirits.

Although these methods satisfied some people that ghosts are real, they did not generate concrete, scientific proof, and most scientists refused to accept the existence of ghosts. However, as scientists in the twentieth century developed more sophisticated instruments for measuring all kinds of physical effects, ghost hunters began to see a way to use these instruments to help them in their quest to prove that ghosts—and haunted houses—do exist. In the following viewpoint, ghost hunter Randolph W. Liebeck describes some of the sophisticated tools in the modern ghost hunter's toolbox.

Liebeck is a career law enforcement officer, a paranormal investigator, and the New Jersey state coordinator for the Ghost Research Society, a national organization. He has also been a consultant on ghosts and hauntings for several television programs.

There are two ways to spot a ghost: 1) wait for one to float up your basement stairs and say "boo," or 2) get the latest equipment and start ghostbusting. For more than 100 years, professional paranormal investigators and the merely curious have looked for the edge that would help them hunt this most elusive game. With recent technological advances, Casper may be in the cross-hairs.

Scientific ghosthunting devices first appeared on the scene in 1882, when the Society for Psychical Research was founded in London. While the introduction of the scientific method heralded the use of investigative tools such as controlled experimentation and photography, the state of the art in paranormal investigations remained fairly stagnant for the next hundred years. Investigators relied mostly on psychics and eyewitnesses. These approaches, while valid information-gathering techniques, leave much to be desired from an evidentiary point of view. Primitive scientific equipment did exist, and it was capable of monitoring and documenting anomalous phenomena, but size, portability, and expense kept such devices out of the hands of field investigators.

The field changed dramatically in the 1980s with rapid advances in microchip technology, computer miniaturization, and dramatic price decreases in high-tech equipment. As new scientific tools were developed to detect environmental changes—mainly for the medical, electronics, and safety industries—paranormal investigators started using them at haunted sites. The practice of using different monitoring and recording devices is based on the assumption that any object or force that interacts with our physical environment will alter that environment in some way.

Several years of experimenting have taught us that unusual measurements can be documented at many haunted locations.

While we have yet to develop a definitive specter-detector or poltergeist energy meter—mainly because we are still not sure what ghosts are made of—a wide range of practical and portable "ghost detection" devices are now available to the paranormal investigator.

## Electromagnetic Field (EMF) Meters

Anomalous electromagnetic-field readings are often recorded in haunted areas. Varying levels of electromagnetism are normal, generated by electric appliances, wiring, overhead powerlines, and the like. Normal electromagnetic fields need to be isolated and ruled out—though it should be noted that some researchers, including William Roll, believe that strong artificial sources of EMF can induce or aggravate poltergeist activity.

Paranormal EMFs are untraceable, fluctuate in intensity, and typically move from one spot to another. They often occupy specifically defined areas of isolated, suspended space, as opposed to emanating from a structural surface. The locations of these pockets may correspond to the exact areas where a psychic claims to see an apparition. Their location and intensity can both be logged by hand-held magnetometers. One low-cost unit, the Tri-field Meter, is routinely used by ghost investigators.

Strong EMFs can also affect magnetic videotape, causing interference bands and resulting in strange glowing or fogged images on tape that are invisible to the naked eye. Similar sound distortions, as well as strange voices, called electronic voice phenomena can show up on magnetic audiotape.

## Radiation Meters

Abnormally high readings of gamma radiation have been detected at some haunted locations. In some cases, geiger counter probes have recorded significant increases in ionizing radiation where psychics claim to see ghosts.

## Thermal Imaging

Thermal imaging cameras, developed for the medical and manufacturing fields, record and display images of objects based on their heat output, as opposed to their ability to reflect light. Using a false-color imaging template, colder areas show up as darker colors and warm areas as lighter colors, registering temperature variations as small as one degree Fahrenheit.

Investigators first used thermal cameras in haunted houses, with successful results, to photograph the anomalous cold spots that they often encountered. An unexpected development has been the detection and filming of unexplained hot spots, both stationary (on a structural surface) and freefloating. As with EMF and ionizing radiation fields, these hot spots often correspond with the exact location a psychic will see or sense an apparition. Interestingly, investigators who place their hands into these hot spots often report a cold sensation.

Color thermal imagers are still out of the reach of most ghosthunters, with prices in the $50,000 range. Most often, television shows such as *Sightings* rent or borrow the imagers to film a field investigation. Less expensive ($8,000) black-and-white imagers, developed for police and firefighting applications, are not sensitive enough for paranormal investigations.

## Night Vision Devices

The military developed light-intensifying lenses for night surveillance. With their stark, green-glowing image field, these units will not work in absolute darkness, but will electronically amplify minute levels of available light (such as moonlight or starlight) to provide a functional image where unaided eyesight or photography would be useless. This allows late-night surveillance in a haunted house without having to turn the lights on. Some ghostly phenomena are reported to be more active at night, and the use of artificial lighting might inhibit a paranormal event. Night vision devices have also allowed investigators to film misty or vaporous manifestations that would have appeared washed-out or invisible under illuminated conditions.

## Thermometers

Short of using expensive thermal imaging units, the best way to document a paranormal cold spot is with a rapid-reading electronic thermometer. (Forget the old mercury-filled tubes.) The best type will give a constant background reading of the room and have an external probe that can be directly inserted into a cold spot. Many units will record and store data continuously, and some can be programmed to sound an alarm if the temperature drops or rises beyond set parameters.

## A Definitive Answer?

While we have yet to come up with a piece of equipment that can prove the existence of a ghost (just what is a ghost?), we can detect and document the unexplained environmental changes that occur in haunted locations. We have made more discoveries and compiled more evidence in the past 16 years than in the entire history of organized ghost research. As science and technology continue to advance, it is not unreasonable to hope that within our lifetime we will be able to define, categorize, and positively establish the existence of ghosts.

# Chapter 2

Fact or Fiction?

# Evidence Against
# Haunted Houses

# A Ghost Hunt Yields No Specters

Margaret Mittelbach and Michael Crewdson

What happens during a modern haunting investigation? Margaret Mittelbach and Michael Crewdson, the authors of the following viewpoint, decided to find out. They made arrangements to participate in an investigation of the reputedly haunted Burlington County Prison in Mount Holly, New Jersey. The investigation was being conducted by South Jersey Ghost Research, a ghost-hunting organization. The ghost hunters avidly used all kinds of technical equipment, hoping to acquire scientific proof that ghosts inhabited the prison, but Mittelbach and Crewdson found that little out of the ordinary seemed to occur. They clearly thought the night's events were a little silly. Mittelbach and Crewdson are the authors of *Wild New York: A Guide to the Wildlife, Wild Places, and Natural Phenomena of New York City.*

We decided we wanted to go ghost hunting. The Ghost Hunting 101 manual, which we found on the Internet, advised against beginners seeking out ghosts on their own. So we contacted the author, the New Jersey–based ghost hunter Dave Juliano, to ask how we should proceed.

Mr. Juliano is the creator of a Web site devoted to the paranormal (www.theshadowlands.net/southjersey) and the co-director of South Jersey Ghost Research, a ghost-hunting club with 35 active members and dozens of affiliate clubs around the country. Its members identify places with possible hauntings (cemeteries, old houses, historic battlefields) and organize investigations using audiovisual and other equipment. Their goal is to bring back proof that ghosts exist.

On the Shadowlands Web site, the club receives about 400 queries a week from people who think their homes are haunted. "[October] is a busy time of year for us," said Mr. Juliano. "We're booked through January for every weekend."

October is busy for the ghost business in general. A ghost-hunting group in Los Angeles has been charging people to participate in an "investigation" of a haunted theater on Hollywood Boulevard. And the Philadelphia Ghost Hunters Alliance has been holding sold-out seminars on "the what, why and where of the spirit realm" in a historic haunted mansion. On a recent Friday night, we accepted Mr. Juliano's invitation to join his club in its investigation of the Burlington County Prison in Mount Holly, N.J. Before the prison was closed in 1965, guards reportedly had seen cigarettes floating in midair in one of the supposedly empty cells. As for the rest of the ghostly activity, Mr. Juliano said it was best to keep us in the dark until we arrived.

Driving toward Mount Holly on the New Jersey Turnpike, we wondered how we would respond if we actually saw something. What if a transparent apparition, dragging a rusty ball and chain, walked up to one of us and tried to bum a smoke?

## The Ghost Hunters

Shortly after exiting the turnpike we found ourselves on a road lined with old red-brick mansions with columned porticos. In the darkness we felt as if we had passed through a portal and entered an early-19th-century village. The prison was hard to miss. It is a handsome gray stone building with iron bars over its windows. Out front we spotted Mr. Juliano, a stocky 31-year-old with a shaved head, directing a group of about 15 people laden with equipment.

Each ghost hunter wore a photo identification badge with name and rank, "investigator" or "team leader." A few had crucifixes carefully positioned outside their shirts, and many were dressed completely in black. If their ID's hadn't read "South Jersey Ghost Research," Mr. Juliano and his crew members might have been mistaken for a bomb squad.

As the ghost hunters filed through the heavy, oak-paneled front doorway, we took a moment to admire the building. Above the entryway "prison" is chiseled in stone, flanked on each side by a carving of skeleton keys surrounded by chains. Scheduled to open as a museum in March, the prison is being restored to look as it did when it opened in 1810.

From Prison Museum Association members, who were observing the proceedings, we learned that the Boston strangler once spent the night here and that executions were performed in the prison's backyard. Some people consider the building to be haunted, and South Jersey Ghost Research was given three hours to see what it could find.

Mr. Juliano, a refrigeration and heating technician by trade, came well prepared. His metal briefcase was packed with equipment: tape recorders, digital cameras, red-beamed flashlights, electromagnetic field detectors (or E.M.F.'s), temperature gauges, walkie-talkies, extra batteries and laminated cards with a prayer to St. Michael asking for his "protection against wickedness and the snares of the Devil."

## The Investigation

Inside the chilly stone walls, cells with doors of iron lined each of the prison's three floors, and a team of investigators was designated for each floor. Mr. Juliano's team set up its equipment on the third floor in a central cell with a vaulted ceiling and a high, tiny window—the death-row cell. "There are legends that you can hear people screaming and wailing," asserted Karen Smith, the coordinator of capital projects for Burlington County. "The people who spent their last days here were shackled by leg irons to a bolt which is embedded in the floor." Among the tales that Ms. Smith has heard is one about the persistent spirit of a man executed in the mid-1800's for killing his wife by bludgeoning her with a table leg. The stories of hauntings began immediately after the murderer was hanged from the prison scaffold.

With the lights on, Mr. Juliano's team set up a night-vision camcorder in one corner of the death-row cell. Electronic sensors, including a motion detector and temperature gauge, were placed strategically around the infamous bolt. If a ghost were even to blink in here, it would be busted.

When the ghost hunters finished setting up their equipment on each floor, the team leaders conferred on walkie-talkies and, in one weird instant, the lights went off throughout the building. "O.K.," said Mr. Juliano. "Let's see what happens."

In the dark the ghost hunters quietly began patrolling the corridors. Some carried E.M.F. detectors, others cameras, others tape recorders. There was even a documentary film crew from Bard College videotaping the search. Outside it began to rain, which added to the creep factor.

"Did you see [the movie] 'The Sixth Sense'?" asked Mr. Juliano in the gloom. "When the little boy in the movie says, 'You know when your hair stands up on the back of your neck? That's them.' That's exactly how I feel when I know something's around. I call it my spider sense; it's a tingling."

We accompanied Mr. Juliano and an investigator, Anne Perlegruto, as they slowly headed from the death-row cell down the right cell block. Mr. Juliano's spider sense soon became activated and it appeared we were stalking something, though we were not sure what. Passing a line of tiny cells with stone walls, Mr. Juliano stopped periodically and quietly said, "Flash," eerily lighting up the whitewashed hallway and grated cell bars with his digital camera.

We ended up in the corner cell, where he got on his walkie-talkie and announced, "Third floor, right wing, last cell, orb photo in the right-hand back corner, where I observed a man walking down the hallway and into the cell." Drat! He had just seen the evening's first ghost, and we missed it completely. Maybe we lacked Mr. Juliano's arachnid sensibilities. We eagerly studied the orb photograph, now stored on his digital camera, which showed a tiny bright dot—or orb—floating in the dark cell. Was this the glowing end of a cigarette?

On past investigations Mr. Juliano and other club members have collected reams of such supernatural evidence (the best of it is posted on their Web site), including photographs of "ectoplasm" (misty vapor), audiotapes of ghost voices (saying things like "help me") and readings of rapidly dropping temperatures (known as cold spots). "I'd rather have a reading on the E.M.F. detector, a temperature drop or a picture than just me saying I see a spirit standing there," said Mr. Juliano. "When you can get all of this evidence together, that's as good as you're going to get short of a ghost going on 'Larry King Live' and saying, 'I'm dead, but I'm here talking to you.'"

Mr. Juliano's determination to prove ghosts are real comes from personal experience. When he was growing up, he spent years seeing ghosts in his parents' house—a glowing, childlike apparition, small black imps, an enormous face speaking from the wall—but no one believed him. "I was terrified," he said. "When this stuff happens to you, you're always questioning your sanity. There was no one to come in and say, 'Yes, there is something happening here, but you don't have Satan living in your basement.'"

## A Moved Cot

Later in the hunt we observed something strange. In the cell next to death row, we noticed that an antique prison cot made of canvas and brass had been moved. When we first saw it, it had been propped up against the wall. Checking again, we found the cot down on the ground as if ready to be slept on.

Hurrying out of the cell, we shared our discovery with the team members stationed on the floor. All denied moving the cot and no one recalled hearing it fall. Blame was quickly shifted to the spirit world. "Objects being moved is very common," explained the team leader, Tome Wilson, in the dim light of the corridor. Mr. Wilson, 21, a fine arts student at York College of Pennsylvania, has had plenty of experience with this phenomenon.

He roomed with a poltergeist for a few months, he said: "It was classic. Doors would slam. Small glass objects would explode. Pictures would come off the walls. Kitchen objects would throw themselves around."

After agreeing that moving a cot is more likely the act of a benign, sleepy spirit than an angry, vengeful one, we marched back into the cell with an E.M.F. detector lent to us by Mr. Juliano. We scanned the cot, but got a normal reading. Strange. We theorized that if there were a ghost here, it had floated off to a quieter place for a nap. Perhaps it was disturbed by the cacophony of two-way radio transmissions and motion-detector alarms accidentally being tripped every few minutes.

We decided to do a little exploring on our own. Heading down steps into a long passageway, we found ourselves in the offices of the future museum. After wandering around in the dark for an hour it was a relief to be in a well-lighted room. The first thing we saw was a perfectly rendered miniature gallows—complete with a tiny noose—displayed on a table.

From that cheery scene, we headed back into the dark and down to the basement where there had been a flurry of activity. We met up again with Mr. Wilson, who told us he had observed a pinkish cloud hovering in the darkness near the doorway to a cell. And when he took flash pictures there with a digital camera, he said, a crescent-shaped ball of light showed up on the images.

The club's other co-director, Jon Williams, 19, showed us a digital orb photograph taken in that area and then told us that an E.M.F. detector stationed in the basement had recorded a highly unusual reading. Apparently the club's psychic investigator, Hildred Robinette, who is retired, had also felt things. She was upstairs where a two-degree drop in temperature in the death-row cell had been recorded.

We went up to investigate. Unlike the other club members, Ms. Robinette did not carry any equipment. She said she had seen ghosts all her life and could even carry on conversations with them. She said she had seen the ghosts of three men in the basement and that one had told her his name, Andrew Morrison.

"There's a lot of anguish here," she said. Even though she seemed a little shaken by her experience, she finally entered the death-row cell just before 11 P.M., and quickly rushed out. "I could see him crouching down," she said, agitated. "He said, 'What are you looking at?' He was real teed off and he didn't want me in there. Then he started cussing at me. He's really a nasty person. I don't like him." We peered into the dark, cramped cell, but received no greeting, nasty or otherwise.

## Where Were the Ghosts?

Although Ms. Robinette seemed to have received a strong impression, we were not the only ones wondering where all the ghosts were. When the three-hour ghost hunt was up, we asked Mr. Wilson how he would rank the ghostly activity here on a scale of 1 to 10. He said: "With 10 being blood dripping from the walls and chandeliers spinning, and 1 being nothing? This place would be a 2."

Packing up at the end of the evening, Mr. Juliano was a bit more optimistic. After all, he considered this simply a preliminary investigation. "I know I saw things and we've heard some stuff, but we have to see what we've captured on video and audio," he said.

We bid adieu to the intrepid ghost hunters and their spectral quarry, and ran from the dark walls of the prison to the comfort of our car. Although our first ghost hunt did not entirely convince us of the existence of the spirit realm, we agreed to keep an open mind. As we prepared to drive away, we noticed that the documentary makers were videotaping our car. Was a ghost making a jailbreak and hitching a ride with us?

On our drive back we mulled over the incident of the cot, the pinkish cloud, the words of the psychic and the mysterious orb photographs. The rain began to pick up even more and finally came down in sheets. Ghosts or no ghosts, we had to admit: it was a dark and stormy night. . . .

# The Borley Rectory "Hauntings" Were Faked

Eric J. Dingwall, Kathleen M. Goldney, and Trevor H. Hall

For many years, Borley Rectory was known as "the most haunted house in England." This was due largely to the publicity generated by Harry Price, an investigator of the paranormal who spent ten years investigating the supposedly haunted rectory and wrote extensively on the events that purportedly occurred there, most notably in his best-selling book *The Most Haunted House in England*.

In 1929, when Price first heard of Borley Rectory, he had been involved in investigating mediums and paranormal phenomena for several years and had founded the National Laboratory of Psychical Research in London. He read an article about the rectory that claimed that strange things happened there and that people saw the ghosts of a medieval nun and a four-horse coach traverse the grounds. In-

Eric J. Dingwall, Kathleen M. Goldney, and Trevor H. Hall, *The Haunting of Borley Rectory*. Glasgow, Scotland: University Press, 1956. Copyright © 1955 by Eric J. Dingwall, Kathleen M. Goldney, and Trevor H. Hall. Reproduced by permission.

trigued, Price made arrangements with the current residents of the rectory, minister G.E. Smith and his wife, to visit the house. Over the course of the nearly one year that the Smiths lived in the rectory, Price visited them several times, investigating the house and its grounds; interviewing the Smiths, their servants, and local townspeople; and participating in séances to try to communicate with the spirits of the ghosts that supposedly lived there. He continued his investigations with the next residents, minister L.A. Foyster and his wife, Marianne. Two years after the Foysters departed, leaving the rectory empty, Price leased the house and set about investigating it more thoroughly.

Price claimed to have conducted one of the most scientific investigations of such a place that had ever been done. But there were those who did not accept his claim. In addition to his other talents, Price was an illusionist; his ability to perform sleight-of-hand tricks raised suspicion in some people's minds. Also, many people thought that Price was a better publicity hound than investigator.

It was not until after his death in 1948 that the strongest criticisms of Price were voiced. By this time, his critics were accusing him of not only sloppy investigation but also falsifying reports and causing some of the poltergeist effects himself. The following selection is from one of the most thorough—and critical—analyses of Price and his methods. The authors—Eric J. Dingwall, Kathleen M. Goldney, and Trevor H. Hall—were members of the Council of the Society for Psychical Research, an English organization unrelated to Price's National Laboratory of Psychical Research and of which Price had been a member at one time. In fact, Price and Dingwall, also an illusionist, had worked together on more than one case investigating mediums, and Price, Dingwall, and Goldney were friends. Their book, like Price's work, was controversial.

In June 1929 the *Daily Mirror* (London) carried a series of articles on the alleged haunting of Borley Rectory in Essex and not far from Long Melford in Suffolk. Through a series of circumstances . . . Price was asked to assist the newspaper's reporter who was at the rectory which was then occupied by the Rev. G. Eric Smith and his wife. As the reporter said in the issue of the *Daily Mirror* for 10 June 1929, all the ingredients of a 'first-class ghost story' were awaiting the investigation of psychic experts. Commenting on the newspaper's invitation, Price, in *The Most Haunted House in England* (henceforward called *MHH*) truly stated that he little dreamt that this first-class ghost story was to 'become the best authenticated case of haunting in the annals of psychical research'. It is clear that at that time he had no idea in his mind that the events at Borley might become a framework around which could be built a dramatic and complex ghost story arrayed in 'scientific' garb. The legend was already there. It had only to be clothed, embellished, and supported by the testimony of others to become alive again. . . . Subsequent events gradually persuaded Price to seize the opportunity with both hands, but it was not before 1940 that his first book on the subject (i.e., *MHH*) was published and created something of a sensation, converting numbers of persons, including, oddly enough, jurists of reputation, to a belief in the paranormal character of the Borley phenomena.

It is on this volume and that subsequently published in London in 1946[1] together with other printed material on Borley, that the present report is based. In addition, however, we have had access to an immense mass of unpublished documents, correspondence, and notes, to which have been added the results of our own enquiries and personal interviews with persons who were involved in the case. As enquiry after enquiry was pursued, it gradually became clear that in the alleged haunting of Borley Rectory we had a case of surpassing interest, not only for the psychical researcher, but also for the student of psychology generally and above all the psychology of testimony and its value under certain unusual conditions. The tale of the Borley haunting developed into a really good ghost story because the legendary skeleton became clothed with a body of material which passed for reality and anything that weakened the flimsy structure was glossed over or treated as of no importance. Normal causes were discounted, critics silenced or their objections overruled, and commonplace happenings were magnified into mysterious and incredible phenomena. *'Everything* is incredible connected with Borley Rectory', wrote Price (*MHH*, p. 152), and even a queer insect seen in the grounds was 'Impossible . . . just one of the many "impossible" things that have happened in this "enchanted" Rectory.'[2]

Price had, it seemed, found at last the repeatable experiment, 'laid on' as it were. 'As a scientist', he wrote, 'I can guarantee you a ghost.'[3]

## Examining Price's Words

Few reviewers, as far as we can ascertain, were bold enough to look behind the façade of suggestion and direct statement put out by Price in *MHH*. But Mr V.S. Pritchett, in the *Bystander* for 23 October 1940, ventured to mention how a Mrs Mansbridge, according to her husband's report of 5 September 1937, 'felt the end of the belt of her coat lifted and dropped again' (*MHH*, p. 233). In Price's version of the incident (p. 128) the belt was 'lifted and dropped again by an unseen hand'. How did Price know that it was a hand, asked Mr Pritchett, adding that no hand had been mentioned by the lady concerned. He forgot that when ghosts are guaranteed, unseen hands must surely be about. . . .

We propose giving the reader a few examples of the materials and methods used in building up the legend.

In cases of this kind it is, of course, useful to maintain that dwellers in the house have had nothing to do with Spiritualism or things psychic. Had they been thus interested it might have been plausibly suggested that their observations and conclusions had possibly been influenced or biased by their beliefs. Thus, in dealing with the life of the Bulls since the rectory was built in 1863, Price states (*MHH*, p. 74) that 'not one of the Bull family, including the Foysters, is concerned with psychical research or spiritualism or knows anything about the subject'. The use of the present tense in this passage is to be especially noted. But even as it stands, the alleged ignorance of those of the Bull family not at that time living in Borley Rectory is somewhat doubtful, considering the interest that their close relations and former rectors of Borley had in the spirits. For example, Price reports that the small summer-house in the garden was often used by the Rev. Henry Bull to commune with the spirits (although this has been denied by a son and daughter in conversation and in writing); and that his son, the Rev. Harry Bull, assured a Mr J. Harley that on many occasions he had himself had personal communications from spirits and that when he died he would, if discontented, adopt devices causing violent physical reactions, such as breaking glass, in order to try to communicate with the inhabitants of the rectory (*MHH*, pp. 25, 50).

A further brief instance may suffice to show how, by omissions from the original reports provided by his observers, Price did not allow readers of his books the opportunity of considering normal causes as an explanation for many of the phenomena. One of Price's principal observers, Mr Mark Kerr-Pearse, in his report dated 26 June 1937 mentioned a

rose tree which was repeatedly blown backwards and for-
wards against the wall causing knocks which 'might provide
an excellent "ghost" for the imaginative'. This observation
may also have been made by another observer, Mr M.
Knox, of University College, Oxford, who, writing to Price on 19
February 1938, stated that he noticed 'several bushes near
the house which might produce a rapping noise against the
walls or windows if the wind blew', and further remarked
that during the night he and his friends heard 'repeated and
distinct thuds or raps, one every ten or twenty seconds',
which they attributed, not to the ghosts, but to the bushes
outside the house. Price did not print the observations of either Mr Kerr-Pearse or Mr Knox, although he mentions
bushes as possible causes of sounds in the 'Blue Book' of instructions [in *MHH*] issued to his corps of observers.

From the above examples, which have been selected from
a much more damaging mass of material . . . it will be seen
how Price built up the case for the Borley haunting. But before closing this brief introduction to our report on Borley,
a word must be said on Price's scheme, formulated in 1937,
by which independent observers should visit Borley and report their findings.[4]

## Influencing the Observers

In any scientific investigation of an alleged haunted house, it
might be thought that the assistance of persons who had already had at least some experience in psychical research
would have been sought. After all, the ordinary person, however intelligent, careful, and acute he may be, cannot be expected to know of or appreciate fully the very many pitfalls
into which even the most experienced psychical researcher
occasionally falls. In the majority of cases the layman knows
little of the scope and range of hallucinatory phenomena,
and is often unable to recognise that kind of abnormal oc-

currence which the expert knows at once should receive special attention. If, on the other hand, what was wanted was bricks to build a good story, at least two points were to be favoured, (a) that the observers should know little about psychical research or the investigation of the alleged phenomena and (b) that they should receive every kind of suggestion as to what they might see, hear, or feel. This was, then, the plan which Price in May 1937 began to put into operation. He inserted an advertisement in *The Times* of 25 May 1937 in which he asked for the assistance of 'responsible persons of leisure and intelligence, intrepid, critical and unbiassed'. 'Scientific training' was, the advertisement stated, 'an advantage', and a private car was essential.

In discussing this plan Price stated that if these observers 'knew nothing about psychical research, so much the better' (*MHH*, p. 106). To each of the observers who was chosen, certain conditions were indicated. Each had to be interviewed by Price; each had to sign a Declaration Form and receive a copy of the Blue Book of instructions,[5] in which was printed an account of the phenomena which, it was asserted, had been seen or heard in Borley Rectory for over forty years. Thus it was suggested to the visitors that the bells mysteriously rang; objects moved from previously determined positions; footsteps, heavy or soft, pattering or shuffling, were heard; knockings, lights, perfumes, apports, apparitions, and other phenomena might be experienced. On the other hand, the observers were told to make 'the greatest effort' to ascertain whether the phenomena were due to normal causes, among which were included rats and farm animals nosing at doors, a factor which must have been inserted by Price for some good reason, although we have neither found any such occurrence reported by any observer nor any reference to its possibility.

The influence of suggestion on the investigation of

haunted houses cannot be exaggerated. In every ordinary house sounds are heard and trivial incidents occur which are unexplained or treated as of no importance. But once the suggestion of the abnormal is put forward—and tentatively accepted—then these incidents become imbued with sinister significance: in fact, they become part of the 'haunt'.

## Messy House, Messy Investigation

Borley Rectory was absolutely ideal for such psychological mechanisms to operate. . . . Here was a great rabbit-warren of a house, cold, draughty, and littered with rubbish, the walls covered with scrawls and squiggles. The very construction of the property, with its peculiar acoustics, favoured the manifestations. And Price took few steps to clear up the muddle and the mess. Indeed, his instructions added to the confusion instead of modifying it. No systematic record or log-book was kept, so that each batch of observers virtually started afresh in total ignorance of what their predecessors had done or what arrangements they had made. Again, it might be thought, in view of the prominence given to the supposed paranormal wall-markings, that Price would have taken the precaution of having at least a couple of walls re-whitewashed. No such thing was done. It was considered sufficient to ring round observed pencil markings and to presume that others found later without a ring were, *ipso facto*, freshly (and paranormally) produced. How faulty any such presumption was is well exemplified by notes written by Major the Hon. Henry Douglas-Home, who visited Borley and recorded as follows after reading *MHH:* 'To show how easy it is, in torchlight—or even daylight—to miss pencil marks on a distemper wall—which has been covered with scribbles, circles and dates—one night—a most observant parson friend of mine, my brother & myself, spent the night there. It was *amazing* [twice underlined] the number of small squiggles which the first person *omitted* to see—(we took it in turn each room & the other two followed shoulder to shoulder) . . . No. 1 missed things that Nos. 2 & 3 could see the whole time!!' The more objects left about the greater the confusion, and the greater the confusion the more chance of 'phenomena' being reported.

Without these suggestions in favour of the paranormal little sensational might have been reported, and as it was, some observers experienced nothing out of the ordinary: a fact which, when reported to Price and occasionally coupled with some mild criticism, was received with but little appreciation. The stock reply to all such objections was that one had to wait for phenomena to occur and stay in the house day by day in perfect quietness, watching and waiting. Moreover, Price added, the phenomena at Borley were 'stronger and more frequent' when the place was occupied by a family. But even these conditions were sometimes met and yet nothing happened. The Rev. Somerset E. Pennefather rented the house towards 1895 for six weeks in the summer. So far as was known by his son, Mr W.S. Pennefather, nothing strange or abnormal occurred. This statement is brushed aside by Price, since, he said, it would be difficult to remember trivial but unusual happenings after forty-five years. Had anything been remembered which would have supported the legend, we may be sure that it would have found a place in *MHH*.

Similarly, Canon H. Lawton[6] wrote to the *Spectator* in 1940 (p. 390) saying that in 1933 he and his family lived in the rectory for a month during the summer and never saw or heard anything out of the ordinary. Canon Lawton, whom we have interviewed . . . actually found and read the MS. [manuscript] written by the Rev. L.A. Foyster in which he described the amazing phenomena said to occur during his incumbency. Canon Lawton, however, who struck us as an extremely reliable and level-headed person and not at all suggestible, said nothing to his wife and during their stay they heard none of the bangs, thuds, or footsteps, or if they did, ascribed them to the normal accompaniments of life in a big country house with the doors and windows open. The Canon's experiences were treated by Price just as he had treated those of Mr Pennefather. To him these gentlemen were merely unlucky, inasmuch as either they proved immune to the psychic influences which permeated the very air of the most haunted house in England or those same influences remained in abeyance during their sojourn there.

## Planted Ideas

From the few examples given above, the reader may get some idea of how the ground was laid for what was to follow and how the minds of the observers were prepared for the reception of just those ideas which Price wanted to plant therein. . . .

When it was over and the connected story printed and published, its reception must have surprised even Price himself. Sir Albion Richardson, the eminent jurist, declared that the manifestations were proved by the evidence to the point of moral certainty (see *EBR*, p. 325) and Sir Ernest Jelf, then Senior Master of the Supreme Court, in discussing the case in the *Law Times* of 9 August 1941, stated that he was at a 'loss to understand what cross-examination could possibly shake it' (*EBR*, p. 323). Sir Ernest's article reveals a strange inability to understand what constitutes valid evidence *in cases of this kind*. It will be part of our task . . . to try to indicate how material of this sort is to be appraised, to show how one fact is to be weighed against another, and how the whole of the evidence must be considered against a background of wilful deception, incompetent investigation, and a barrage of suggestion directed against the observers, many of whom seem to have been chosen with at least one qualification: that is to say, a lack of acquaintance with the technical methods to be used in the enquiry with which they were expected to deal.

## Notes

1. *The End of Borley Rectory* (henceforward called *EBR*).
2. *MHH*, p. 136.
3. *Listener,* 10 November 1937, p. 1014.
4. See *MHH*, pp. 116 ff.
5. See *MHH*, pp. 193 ff.
6. Hon. Canon of Manchester Cathedral (1950–53) and now (1954) Hon. Canon and Sub-Dean of the Pro-Cathedral at Buenos Aires.

# The "Haunting" of Toronto's Mackenzie House Is Easily Explained

Joe Nickell with John F. Fischer

One of Canada's best-known haunted houses is Mackenzie House in Toronto, Ontario. The old brick mansion was the last home of William Lyon Mackenzie, who as a young man of twenty-five emigrated to Canada from Scotland in 1820. Mackenzie published the *Colonial Advocate*, a political newspaper, and actively campaigned for Canada's liberty from England. At one point, he even led on abortive coup against the government; he was captured, imprisoned for treason, and eventually freed. Mackenzie's final years "were full of bitterness over his failed political ambitions and his financial difficulties," according to Michael Norman and Beth Scott in *Haunted America*. Indeed, his financial straits were so severe that friends purchased for him the mansion that

Joe Nickell with John F. Fischer, *Secrets of the Supernatural: Investigating the World's Occult Mysteries*. Amherst, NY: Prometheus Books, 1991. Copyright © 1988 by Joe Nickell. All rights reserved. Reproduced by permission.

today bears his name and where he died "an ill-tempered and disillusioned old man," say Norman and Scott. Mackenzie's ghost has reportedly been encountered in the house from time to time, running an old printing press or playing the organ. But more frequently, his wife, Isabel, has been seen walking down the front stairs and out of the house or haunting the kitchen. Some reports say that a priest performed an exorcism there in 1960, putting an end to most of the ghostly manifestations. However, people continue to tour the "haunted" house, now operated as a museum, and claim to hear ghostly footsteps and to experience other strange things.

The following viewpoint about Mackenzie House was written by Joe Nickell and John F. Fischer, well-known forensic scientists. Nickell is a prominent member of the Committee for the Scientific Investigation of Claims of the Paranormal (CSICOP), an organization known for its skepticism about the paranormal. He writes a regular column for the *Skeptical Inquirer*, CSICOP's journal, and is the author of numerous articles and books, including *Camera Clues: A Handbook of Photographic Investigation, Real-Life X-Files: Investigating the Paranormal*, and *Entities: Angels, Spirits, Demons, and Other Alien Beings*. Before his death in 2002, Fischer was a forensic analyst with a Florida crime laboratory and a scientific and technical adviser to CSICOP. The two men collaborated on three books, *Secrets of the Supernatural: Investigating the World's Occult Mysteries, Mysterious Realms: Probing Paranormal, Historical, and Forensic Enigmas*, and *Crime Science: Methods of Forensic Detection*.

In the following selection, they review the history of Mackenzie House and the reports of the ghostly events there. Then Nickell tells about his own visit to the mansion, during which he found evidence that the alleged haunting is nonsense.

$A$ century after his death, the ghost of Toronto's rebel-statesman, William Lyon Mackenzie, was not merely going "bump in the night" but, according to several accounts, was also treading noisily upon the stairs of his historic home, plunking the keys of the parlor piano, and even managing to operate his antique printing press—although it was locked and rusting in the cellar![1]

Mackenzie seems a fitting candidate for ghosthood—particularly ghosthood of the restless type—given his turbulent past. Born in 1795 in Scotland, Mackenzie later emigrated to Canada and became a shopkeeper in Toronto (then the town of York). He published the *Colonial Advocate*, a newspaper which served as a vehicle for his attacks against the governing clique. These articles made him a popular hero on the political front, and he was soon elected (1828), then five times re-elected, to the Legislative Assembly of Upper Canada. In 1834 he became Toronto's first civic mayor.

In 1837 Mackenzie led a group of some eight hundred Toronto insurrectionists with the intention of setting up a provisional government. Failing this, he fled to the United States, nearly provoking a war between the two countries before finally being imprisoned (until 1840) for violating American neutrality laws. He eventually succeeded in drawing Britain's attention to colonial abuses, and served again in parliament from 1851 to 1858. He died in 1861 in the now historic—and supposedly haunted—house on Bond Street.

## Caretaker's Tales

The story of the spooky shenanigans became known in 1960 when Mr. and Mrs. Alex Dobban—who had been caretakers at Mackenzie House for just over a month—told their story to the *Toronto Telegram* and attested to certain ghostly events in sworn statements.

Subsequently an army pensioner and his wife Mr. and Mrs. Charles Edmunds, came forward with tales of additional happenings. They had been caretakers of Mackenzie House from August 1956 until April 1960. As Mrs. Edmunds told the *Telegram*, she often saw a woman, or sometimes a small man in a frock coat, standing in her room. For example:

> One night I woke up at midnight to see a lady standing over my bed. She wasn't at the side, but at the head of the bed, leaning over me. There is no room for anyone to stand where she was. The bed is pushed against the wall. She was hanging down like a shadow but I could see her clearly. Something seemed to touch me on the shoulder to wake me up. She had long hair hanging down in front of her shoulders. . . . She had a long narrow face. Then she was gone.[2]

As ghostly occurrences go, however, Mrs. Edmunds's visions are of a type of that is all too common. Indeed, they match a phenomenon psychologists term hypnopompic hallucinations. Often described as "waking dreams," such visions are frequently of the ghost-at-the bedside variety.[3] In fact, Mrs. Edmunds's husband had told her she was dreaming.[4] Yet, in a later statement, he said:

> Another night my wife woke up and woke me. She was upset. She said the lady had hit her. There were three red welts on the left side of her face. They were like finger marks. The next day her eye was bloodshot. Then it turned black and blue. Something had hit her.

And then, as if anticipating the skeptic, Charles Edmunds insisted: "It wasn't me. I don't think she could have done it herself."[5] Yet who is to say that one of them—tossing fitfully in sleep—did not in fact accidentally strike a swiping blow to Mrs. Edmunds's face?

Subsequent events developed into a full-blown case of

what psychologists term "contagion"[6]—a sort of bandwagon effect, which can best be illustrated with the following (non-haunting) example. On December 10, 1978, a
small panda escaped from its shelter in the Blijdorp Zoo in
Rotterdam, Holland. No sooner did a newspaper report the
loss than phone calls began to come in. There were repeated
sightings from across the Netherlands, their number under-
scored by the fact that the panda had actually traveled just
500 meters to a railroad track where it had been killed, presumably by a passing train.[7] As to the panda sightings, probably some persons had seen other animals which they mis-
took for the missing creature. Others may have perceived a
movement out of the corner of the eye and have honestly
thought they "saw" what they expected to see. Still other
calls may have been pranks or hoaxes.

In the case of Mackenzie House, the Edmunds's visiting
grandchildren, ages three and four, were soon claiming they
had seen a ghost. After the caretakers moved out, Toronto
newspapers hyped the story. *Telegram* reporter Andy Mac-
Farlane and photographer Joe Black gained permission to
spend a night in the house, but they were skeptics and experienced nothing.

Nevertheless Archdeacon John Frank of the Holy Trinity
Church performed the rites of exorcism in the house, concluding: ". . . Look Down, O Lord, from thy heavenly throne,
illuminate the darkness of this night with Thy celestial
brightness, and from the sons of light banish the deeds of
darkness: through Jesus Christ our Lord. Amen."[8]

In January of the following year, *Fate* magazine carried
the story of the alleged haunting. And in 1962, renovations
on the house brought reports from workmen who claimed
that a sawhorse and dropsheets had been unaccountably
moved in the night, although a later break-in and theft
seemed less mysterious. Another incident suggested that the

workmen, who were obviously caught up in the brouhaha, were playing pranks on each other. One of the men encountered a hangman's noose that had been placed over the stairway.[9]

In 1968 Susy Smith—who would later write of the ghost story at chapter length in her *Ghosts Around the House* (1970)—visited the site. That was on November 1—or, as she observes, "All Hallows," adding that she had spent Halloween with "a cult of hippie witches." Indeed, she had brought with her to Mackenzie House two "warlocks" known as Raji and J.C. Ms. Smith did admit that the pair "were usually high" on marijuana or hashish, which may explain how they were able to perceive ghosts even when there were none. For example, in descending Mackenzie House's steep staircase, Ms. Smith admitted that she "tripped and nearly fell on my face," but Raji claimed a "demon" had given her a push, while J.C. maintained that "an unseen ghost" was the culprit.[10]

In another instance, Ms. Smith states that "whatever it was . . . knocked my camera off a table . . . and dented it badly. I presumed I had just laid the camera carelessly so that it became overbalanced; but Raji said it was pushed by a demon. J.C. insisted it was an unseen ghost."

Nevertheless, she managed to obtain a spooky picture. The published photo shows Raji with his fingers extended over the keyboard of the antique piano. As Susy Smith herself describes it, it ". . . reveals a mysterious kind of mist between his hands and the keys. If this was caused by double exposure, why is not the rest of the picture in duplicate?"

The answer, of course, is that double exposure was not involved; neither, probably, was camera damage. The answer is so simple and obvious that one would have thought a supposed investigator like Susy Smith could have discovered it. The "mist" is merely the result of glare—or "flashback," as it is sometimes called. The white pages of music resting on the piano simply bounced back her flash, thus washing out a portion of the picture. (As further substantiation, even the dark—albeit polished—wood of the piano shines around the music sheets. And in conjunction, of course, extreme shadows are also present in the print.) I showed the published photograph to a professional photographer, and he concurred with my explanation of the "mist."[11] Susy Smith, however, says nothing about seeking an expert opinion.

## Haunting Phenomena

Despite an early debunking by the *Star*, the circus atmosphere at Mackenzie House prevailed off and on for some eight years.

In a 1960 editorial, the newspaper attributed the initial reports of ghostly goings-on to the imagination of a publicist for the nonprofit Mackenzie Homestead Foundation. Alex Dobban had said of the ghostly occurrences, according to the newspaper, that there was "nothing to it." He also maintained that his reasons for moving out of the house had had nothing to do with spooks.[12]

Nevertheless, both the Dobbans and the Edmundses had reported some distinctive phenomena which were also experienced by others. From an investigative standpoint such occurrences are the most interesting because they could indicate some reality beyond dreams, imagination, or hype.

Both Mr. Edmunds and his wife, for example, claimed to hear footsteps on the stairs. As Mr. Edmunds stated, "They were thumping footsteps like someone with heavy boots. This happened frequently when there was no one in the house but us, when we were sitting together upstairs." They also reported peculiar rumbling noises. Their son Robert (who, together with his wife and two small children, lived at the house for a period) described the sound as a rumbling and clanking. He likened it to that made by old printing presses that he had seen in movies. "Not like modern presses," he insisted. Although the younger Edmunds couple heard the "press" but a single time, they maintained that they heard the piano play on some three or four occasions.

During their nerve-wracking tenancy at Mackenzie House, the elder Mrs. Edmunds reportedly lost 40 pounds, and eventually she and her husband moved out. In moved Mr. and Mrs. Dobban, but after scarcely a month they, too, gave up the ghost. As Mrs. Dobban stated in her affidavit:

> We hadn't been here long when I heard footsteps going up the stairs. I called to my husband, but he wasn't there. There was no one else in the house—but I definitely heard feet on the stairs.

She added:

> One night I woke up. There was a rumbling noise in the basement. At first I took it to be the oil burner; but my husband checked and the furnace wasn't on. As it turned out, the noise I heard was the press. It's locked, but I heard it running, not only that night but one or two other nights as well.

She went on to say that another time, when she and her husband had been in bed, she had heard the antique piano playing in the parlor downstairs—not a *tune*, but random plunkings as if a child were playfully hitting on the keys. Robert Edmunds had also heard the weird performance: "I cannot remember what the music was like," he said, "but it was the piano downstairs playing."[13]

## The Author's Investigation Begins

Such phenomena invited investigation, and I accepted the challenge during 1972–73 while living in Toronto and working as a professional stage magician. I had been writing a skeptical column on mysterious phenomena—"poltergeists," a spurious "mummy" of a "devil baby," and the like, some of which I had personally begun to investigate—for a magicians' magazine. (At the time I was also studying criminalistics and investigative methods, and would subsequently become a licensed investigator for an international detective agency.)

Before paying a first visit to the house, I searched out published material on the case—old newspaper clippings, books, and magazine articles. In the course of my research I became aware of a surprising lack of concern with the building's environs, all the more so since I had learned that next door to the 82 Bond Street address was Macmillan and Company, the book publishing firm. Could late-night press operations there, I wondered, account for the unexplained rumbling sounds?

The answer, in fact, was no. As my friend, Toronto writer Doug Fetherling, assured me (Macmillan having been his publisher), the building was a combination of offices and warehouse; the printing took place elsewhere. I decided the time had come to see the Mackenzie Homestead firsthand.

Like other visitors, I was greeted by a hostess in period costume who guided me through the narrow dwelling. In the parlor she pointed out an oil portrait of William Lyon Mackenzie, the old family album, and of course the little antique piano. The cellar no longer held the printing press, which had been restored and now reposed, along with Mackenzie's old desk and red leather chair, in a wing added at the rear of the house.

I learned from my guide that caretakers no longer lived there, but that, even so, current policy forbade anyone to spend the night there. I questioned her about her own experiences. She had seen no ghost but in fact *had* heard the mysterious footfalls on the staircase. However, she had managed, on one occasion, to reach the stairs while the phenomenon was still in progress and had learned the source: The sounds were coming from the adjacent Macmillan building.[14] Mackenzie House is separated from Macmillan by only the narrowest walkway. Directly opposite the Mackenzie staircase is a parallel one of Macmillan's. Indeed the latter is made of iron, which amplifies the sound of footsteps—most noticeably those made by the night crew, while caretakers were lying quietly abed thinking of ghosts. According to the hostess, the sense that the footsteps were coming from somewhere within the house was a most convincing illusion.

On a later occasion I visited Macmillan's. In speaking with a receptionist and an editor, I learned that the only printing equipment on the premises was a large mimeograph machine which, although located in a room adjacent to Mackenzie Homestead, was never used at night.

Despite such negative responses, I wanted to talk to the Macmillan building's superintendent. I wondered what he thought of the strange goings-on next door, whether he knew of the part played by the iron staircase in the affair, and whether he had heard the rumbling noises or had any explanation for them.

Luckily, his tenure extended back to the earlier disturbances. As Macmillan personnel introduced him to me, he asked (rather mischievously, I thought) whether I believed in ghosts. I told him I was skeptical, that I believed that most reported ghostly occurrences had rather simple explanations, and that these should be eliminated before we invoked the supernatural. He nodded, but—his eyes twinkling—he stated that he knew one of the Mackenzie House ghosts "personally." If I would return after work in the early evening and ring the bell a specified number of times, he would, he promised, reveal all to my satisfaction. It was an offer I could not refuse.

## A Neighbor's Revelations

Shortly before the appointed time, I stood outside Mackenzie House, listening intently. Almost at once I began to hear a faint, distant rumbling—not thunder, but a metallic, machine-like sound not unlike an antique printing press. The sound grew: it was the Dundas Street trolley. I doubted this was actually the source of the reported rumblings, but it did inspire some further thought. Since there was a subway station not far away, I wondered whether the sounds of the underground train might be conducted along sewers or pipes to the celler of Mackenzie House. With that thought in mind, I kept my appointment with the enigmatic custodian.

After greeting me at the door, he led the way into the basement warehouse. Saying somewhat cryptically that he wished to try something, he left me standing at a spot near the Mackenzie cellar while he scurried away. Soon there emerged from the shadows strange noises—eerie whines and clunks and clanks and rumbles. Before long, the "super" was back, wanting to know if I had heard anything mysterious. He explained that he had simply turned on the boiler and—as I had begun to guess—the sounds were caused by the network of expanding pipes.[15]

For his next demonstration, he brought out a large, flat-bedded cart equipped with heavy iron wheels. Loading it with metal garbage cans, as was typically done by the late-night clean-up crew, he pushed it across the warehouse's rough concrete floor. It rumbled and clattered noisily. As the superintendent explained, due to the proximity of the two buildings and their steel underpinnings, the sounds would be telegraphed next door. From the upstairs rooms of the caretakers, *presto*: an antique printing press, surely operated by old Mackenzie himself!

My guide now led me up the offending iron staircase, and explained its proximity to the Mackenzie one, basically corroborating what the hostess there had observed. His was independent confirmation, since I had avoided telling him anything she had said.

I asked about the piano. I had begun to wonder to myself whether the eerie sounds of the expanding or contracting pipes might have seemed—to a suggestible person—like someone plunking, childlike, at the old keyboard. However, I was told that to account for the sounds of the piano we would have to continue on up to the roof.

As it turned out, his family's apartment jutted above the flat expanse of the rest of the Macmillan building. He explained how his son's piano music wafted across the flat roof, struck the taller brick house, and was consequently amplified by a sort of echo-chamber effect caused by the space between the two buildings. Privately, the custodian had determined that such sounds actually seemed louder inside the house due to the effect of the amplification.

My tour ended with the super casually noting a noisy ventilator fan as he led me to his family's quarters. Over a cup of his wife's coffee I heard another little tale concerning the "ghost" of Mackenzie House. One night the custodian was drawn to the rear of the historic dwelling by voices of what turned out to be a group of college kids. Using a listening device which they had placed against the rear wall, they were certain, they told him, that they were hearing spooky manifestations. He donned the earphones, listened briefly, then laughed. "Boys, I hate to tell you, but your 'ghost' is the automatic flush on the men's urinal next door!"[16]

I was left with only one further question for my host. Why, with all the publicity over the alleged haunting, had he not come forward with his own knowledge of the sources of the phenomena? He replied simply that no one—neither self-styled "ghost hunter" nor reporter nor even curiosity seeker—had ever bothered to inquire next door. He had decided, apparently bemusedly, to wait until someone did. It had taken a dozen years.

## Notes

1. An earlier article on the alleged haunting is Joe Nickell, "The Ghost at Mackenzie House," *Canada West*, Fall 1979, 16–18. Other, less skeptical accounts are in Sheila Hervey, *Some Canadian Ghosts* (Richmond Hill, Ontario: Simon & Schuster of Canada, 1973), 106–114, and Susy Smith, "Turbulence in Toronto," chap. 2 in *Ghosts Around the House* (New York: World Publishing, 1970), 38–50.

2. Mrs. Edmunds's statement to the *Toronto Telegram* is given in Smith, "Turbulence in Toronto," 44.

3. Robert A. Baker, Professor of Psychology, lecture on "ghost-busting," University of Kentucky, 30 October 1987.

4. Quoted in Smith, "Turbulence in Toronto," 46.

5. Ibid.

6. Rom Harré and Roger Lamb, "Contagion," in *The Encyclopedic Dictionary of Psychology* (Cambridge, Mass.: MIT Press, 1983), 119.

7. Hans van Kampen, "The Case of the Lost Panda," *Skeptical Inquirer* 4, no. 1 (Fall 1979): 48–50.

8. Hervey, *Some Canadian Ghosts*, 110–114.

9. Ibid.

10. Smith, "Turbulence in Toronto," 38.

11. Felix Glied, personal communication, cited in Nickell, "The Ghost at Mackenzie House," 17.

12. Editorial, *Toronto Daily Star*, 28 June 1960; portions cited in Hervey, *Some Canadian Ghosts*, 110–111.

13. Smith, "Turbulence in Toronto," 43–47; Hervey, *Some Canadian Ghosts*, 107–109. See also Richard Winer and Nancy Osborn, *Haunted Houses* (New York: Bantam, 1979), 133–135.

14. Mackenzie Homestead tour guide, personal communication, 21 August 1972.

15. Tony Vrewey, personal communication, 8 May 1973.

16. Ibid.

# The Amityville "Haunting" Was a Hoax

Loyd Auerbach

In December 1975, George and Kathleen Lutz and their three children moved into a pleasant Dutch colonial home in suburban Amityville on Long Island, New York. They knew when they purchased the house that only a year earlier, twenty-three-year-old Ron DeFeo had massacred his parents and siblings in the home, which had remained empty until the Lutzes bought it. The Lutzes were unconcerned about the crime, but only a month after moving in they left the house for good. They claimed that they had been forced to leave because of the terrifying demonic events that occurred there.

Two years later, the Lutzes' experiences were recounted in a best-selling book, *The Amityville Horror* by Jay Anson, and shortly after that a hit movie with the same name arrived on the big screen. The book purported to be nonfiction; its horrific description of the Lutzes' short stay in the house supposedly told the factual story of what had happened. However, almost from the beginning, questions were raised about the truthfulness of the tale. As Loyd Auerbach, author of the following viewpoint, states, the book contained many discrepancies in minor details, such as the weather on a particular day or night, and these discrepancies raised questions about the veracity of the rest of the book. Auerbach recounts some of the information that leads him to agree with those who say the Amityville haunting was a hoax.

Auerbach is director of the Office of Paranormal Investigations and a consulting editor for *FATE*, a publication about the paranormal. He has also written several books about parapsychology and his own experiences in this unusual field.

In 1977, a book was released detailing an incredible series of experiences by a family in Amityville, Long Island, New York. George and Kathy Lutz and their three children had bought what they thought was their dream house in 1975, moved in, and reportedly saw their dream turn into a nightmare. They had bought the house previously inhabited by Ron DeFeo and the family he brutally murdered. Their nightmare was recounted in *The Amityville Horror*, a book written by Jay Anson, which has the words "A True Story" on the front cover.

The family reportedly was attacked by unseen forces that made life in the house a living hell. Physical objects were moved about and broken, green slime oozed from the ceiling, mysterious infestations of flies appeared in the winter, apparitions of piglike and demonic figures were seen. Kathy Lutz was fondled by an invisible entity, music and voices were heard, and the children and their dog acted strangely, just to mention a few things. They even reported that the family priest who visited them had similar experiences. Parapsychologists and media people made many visits to the home after the family moved out, and some "investigators" still talk of their experiences there to this day.

The book was a best-seller, and the film based on it didn't do too badly at the box office either. People believed the Lutz family's story and some were afraid. After all, "if it could happen to an ordinary family like the Lutzes, why not to someone like me?" Both the film and the book did very little to suggest that the story was anything but true, and even the attorney for Ronald DeFeo joined in to say that there were indeed odd goings-on in that house. DeFeo himself had apparently claimed that prior to the murders he had heard voices telling him what to do.

Then, in 1979, William Weber, DeFeo's attorney, decided to change his tune. The "Amityville Horror" was a hoax dreamed up by George and Kathy Lutz and Weber himself, over wine, to cash in on a big opportunity. According to Weber in a July 26, 1979, Associated Press story, "We created this horror story over many bottles of wine that George was drinking. We were really playing with each other. We were creating something the public would want to hear about."

## Conflicting Details

Let's take a closer look back over this case of an apparent hoax perpetrated on the public. Before the film was the book. The film (as films do) made the events more graphic than they appeared in the book, but with both the book and the film claiming to reveal "a true story," it is likely that people who may have actually been having psychic experiences at the time would have been more affected than any others. It is for this reason that people must really understand how such tales can be manufactured and "sold" to the public.

In a book review for the CSICOP [Committee for the Scientific Investigation of Claims of the Paranormal] organization's publication, *The Skeptical Inquirer*, Dr. Robert Morris looked closely at the events detailed in the book. He found several discrepancies within the book itself, contradictions of what was going on in the real world, including wrong weather conditions (the story conflicted with the actual weather reports in the New York area), incorrect dates (such as the date they moved into the house being December 23 as opposed to December 18), and even the name of the Psychical Research Foundation (labeled as the Psychical Research Institute). Granted, these may be minor discrepancies, but when looking at extreme claims of paranormal events, we must scrutinize all information carefully to make sure everything checks out.

An article in *The Washington Post* from September 16, 1979, also focused on such discrepancies, citing a previous article from Long Island's *Newsday*. In the article, entitled "The Calamityville Horror," journalist Michael Kernan points out contradictions such as George Lutz's allegedly learning that their house was located where the Shinnecock Indians put their sick and dying, while the historical records show that the Indian tribe lived nowhere near that spot. Or his report of having seen a pig's face staring at him from a window very early Christmas morning (1975) while the moon was quite full, even though records for that date have the moon in its third quarter and setting well before midnight.

In addition, Kernan reports discrepancies involving people, such as that of the police officer who supposedly investigated denying he'd been on the property. In fact, local police were apparently not contacted until after the Lutzes moved out. But of course all these contradictions could possibly have been due to author Jay Anson, who never even went to visit the house.

Anson also wrote that the house was investigated by parapsychologists. It is true, in fact, that researchers visited the home and spoke with the Lutzes. As it happens, Dr. Karlis Osis of the American Society for Psychical Research [ASPR], and Jerry Solfvin, then with the Psychical Research Foundation in North Carolina, paid a visit, as did another investigator sent by Jerry Solfvin, as well as a few others, such as author Hans Holzer and demonologists Ed and Lorraine Warren. . . .

## What the Parapsychologists Said

I spoke with Jerry Solfvin and Karlis Osis about the Amityville case, since Jerry had eventually gotten to the house for the Psychical Research Foundation, and Dr. Osis for the ASPR.

"In early January 1976, around the twelfth or thirteenth, the family called," said Jerry. "George Lutz called me and told me about the situation. At the time, Bill Roll was out of town and Keith Harary [both were parapsychology researchers] and I were there" at the Psychical Research Foundation. So Keith and I set up a time when he [George Lutz] would call us or we would call him over the next three or four nights. Keith and I would both speak to him about the situation. It seemed interesting, but it wasn't interesting enough for us to make a trip, to go up there and see for ourselves.

"Keith's good friend George Kekoris lived right there on Long Island a few miles away." Jerry and Keith spoke with George Kekoris and asked him if he'd like to investigate a poltergeist case, and "gave him instructions on how to handle it. He had gone with Keith before when they had some sort of haunted house situation and he was somewhat familiar with the literature. So he went over and he collected information, mostly after the family had moved out. They contacted us around the twelfth, thirteenth, of January and it was something like the fifteenth or the twentieth when they moved out. So all of this, meaning the investigations by George [Kekoris], was done after the family moved out." (They actually moved out on January 15, 1976.)

"He went and spoke with the priest that was involved, and spent long hours with the family, and he went over and made a few visits to the house with a couple of friends. They went in and looked around and verified a few things like 'this object was broken by such-and-such, by the wind,' and they saw those objects." But was the Amityville case convincing in terms of its possible paranormal content? No, for according to Jerry, "the whole thing stacked up as not very interesting. There was nothing objective. It was all the perceptions of the family, all subjective phenomena. All of the things that they told us about, that they told to me or to Keith directly, or told to George, could have been interpreted in a variety of ways. There was no hard evidence of the events whatsoever.

"Some months later, in March, I was visiting the New England area, and I stopped in New York and called the Lutzes." Jerry told them he was in town and that he'd like to stop over and talk with them. "They had moved and they were living a couple of miles away. That was the same afternoon that Alex Tanous came over with Karlis Osis [both were parapsychologists]." Apparently, this was a stroke of luck for Jerry.

"I had a chance to chat with them after Alex and Karlis talked to the family. Alex and Karlis went over to the house first, and I stayed to talk to the family. After about an hour they came back and they sat down and asked questions of the family. They gave the keys back and Alex and I had a chance to go back into a corner and talk."

Alex said something to Jerry on the order of "What do you think of this thing? I don't see anything here. There's nothing here. I think this is a real hoax." According to Dr. Osis, the Lutzes showed a sample of DeFeo's handwriting to them which was on a contract they had in their possession, which Alex got a bit more than a glimpse of. "There was a contract which already outlined the gains from the book and the film," said Dr. Osis. "This was enough for us to indicate what it was. Apparently, they did not imagine that Alex would catch on to it." The signatures were, according to Osis, at the end of the contract, but Alex Tanous was a bit shrewder than they must have imagined. "I didn't see what it was a contract for, but it was pretty evident it was for a film or a book," said Alex. "It was very nice to get out of it," said Osis.

When I recently asked Alex about the situation, he replied, "I never saw anything paranormal in the house. It was all perfectly normal. I'd never seen any of those things happen, there or elsewhere, and I did the actual investigation." Alex also told me that he was quoted by some article later as saying he saw the devil in the house. Untrue.

Jerry went over to the house to see for himself, but when he got there he wasn't alone. "All of a sudden there are these camera crews," he said. "In comes CBS, in comes *The National Enquirer*, in comes Lorraine and Ed Warren. And there must have been like twenty-five people there, zooming around the house with an 'EEK' and screams, and all sorts of crazy stuff like 'I see it! I feel it! Oh I can breathe.' It was like a zoo."

During that period, Jerry Solfvin got a lot of information "from two guys who have a little foundation out in Long Island City. One of them had a radio program where he interviewed people. During that two- or three-day period that I was down there he had me on his program. The contact that I had with him began in early February, possibly late January, but fairly fresh into the case, when people were still wondering. What happened was that this guy really did a bang-up job on the Amityville house. He went in and he took pictures of everything, because he's a photo-journalist. Later I went into his laboratory and it was unbelievable. You could say 'What about that knob on the third drawer down on the left side of the kitchen' and he would have a blowup of it from several angles. He did an unbelievable investigative job of that."

## A Story Made Up over Wine

"His conclusion was, at that time, that it was a hoax. He was the one who informed me about the appearance on WBAI radio of the lawyer for the DeFeo family who came out publicly during that year, after the book had come out but before the movie. He came out and said something like 'I'll tell you about Amityville horror. That story was made up by me and the Lutzes. We sat down over a bottle of apple wine and it was my idea. I approached them with the idea that we could make a bundle of money off this, and that we could have a book and a movie and so forth. Then they went off and did it on their own and I want my half and I'm suing him.'" Jerry's words for what Weber said may not have been exact, but the intent is the same. Weber was indeed suing the Lutzes, while they were attempting a countersuit.

Jay Anson was contracted by Prentice-Hall, and never went to the house himself. "After his first visit to the Lutzes, he was referred to me and to a family priest who was very supportive of them," said Jerry. Apparently, Anson was in bed and "was sick and that's when he was writing the book. He called about every other day and we had really long conversations. He was a really nice fellow, otherwise I wouldn't have done that. It was very clear that he was trying to get me or someone else to make a definite statement that he could put in the book, that 'my investigation had shown . . .' He wanted that very much. So we had long discussions, and he was open about what he wanted, but I couldn't give that to him then or at any other point. ". . .

## A Case Not Eligible for Real Investigation

The misunderstanding was put across by the book that parapsychologists had fully investigated the situation. Given the criteria for deciding if a case is truly investigable—that the case be current, events frequent, and that there be witnesses—the Amityville case does seem to meet them. But there are major glitches here. The Lutz family had already moved out when the investigators came, so the case was barely current, since events, although in the recent past, were no longer going on. An investigator could not see the Lutz family and their reported paranormal occurrences in any semblance of the situational relationships, for the simple reason that they were no longer in the same house.

The events, as reported, had been frequent, but since the family moved out, they were frequent no more, ceasing in the now-empty house. In terms of an actual spontaneous case investigation, then, this would have been a poor case, since there was no chance to see any of the original setup of the situation (the house may have been there, but the family was not). True, an investigator can still add to knowledge about such cases by interviewing witnesses after the fact, but in one like this, as with any, where there is no objective evidence (such as apparitional sightings, where people say they saw an apparition), one can learn as much by observing the interrelationships between the people involved as one could by interviewing them about their experiences.

But as you can see by what Jerry was saying, the testimony of the Lutzes was suspect. Their story was extreme in comparison with previous cases in the history of psychical research, the statements of William Weber raise doubts, to say the least, and Alex Tanous had seen a movie contract. While the Lutzes claimed Weber was wrong, that they had indeed experienced what they claimed, the other points add too much weight to the suspicion that the whole story was a hoax perpetrated for the sake of fortune.

Given that an investigator in this field really needs to eliminate all "normal" factors, including fraud on the part of the witnesses, and given the other factors weighing against their story, we really cannot avoid the conclusion that the events of the Amityville "Horror" were fiction, pure and simple. Certainly it's possible that since the house was the site of a violent and emotional event (the DeFeo killings), it was "haunted," and that the Lutzes picked up on that event (psychically); there have even been poltergeist cases which seem to be connected with hauntings of that kind, which triggers the RSPK ("poltergeistery") of someone living in such a place. But any such interpretation would be stretching the actual evidence for and against the Lutzes' story a bit much, and the likeliest conclusion is still that the case was a hoax.

The case of the "Amityville Horror" is a prime example of how things can be fabricated and blown out of proportion through utilization of the media. Dr. Osis and Alex Tanous avoided the media "circus" that was arriving as they were leaving the house since they did not want to be dragged in to what Jerry Solfvin called a "zoo." That one encounter in the house showed the way people can get further carried away for showmanship's sake, and Osis and Tanous avoided it like the plague. . . .

## Why Hoaxes Like These Happen

It's important for you to understand the reasons why things like this can happen. Well, they happen for a number of reasons. First of all, they happen because people are greedy. . . .

Another cause of something like the Amityville situation

is the media themselves. . . . The media often want what we in parapsychology cannot deliver. They want flashy cases that grab people's attention. Unfortunately, the media people themselves are often less than discriminatory when checking up on what is known about a particular case or how it compares to what parapsychology studies.

Finally, there are those who like to hop on the bandwagon in any "media event" such as this. They may be well-meaning people who do in fact wish to get to the heart, the truth, of the matter, but whose beliefs or method of operating conflict with the methods of science, thereby helping to mix up the explanation of what is really happening. Or they may be people who help keep up the misconceptions presented by horror films and the like, that we are to be in awe of these things, if not scared out of our wits, and that we must call upon these selfsame people to "come to the rescue."

## Beware of Extreme Claims

So beware of extreme claims of the paranormal. Such claims may make wonderful (and not so wonderful) horror books and films, but even when they claim to be "based on a true story," remember that you are reading or seeing a *story*, unless you can dig further to uncover what part of the story was true, if any at all. Anyone and everyone might have a psychic experience, perhaps even an intense one. But anyone and everyone doesn't have experiences like these. In fact, in the history of parapsychological field investigation, no one really has. Outside the realm of fiction, that is.

# There Is No Evidence That Ghosts Exist

Joe Nickell

In the following selection, Joe Nickell argues that so-called hauntings are not genuine. Those who claim to have seen spirits of the undead have actually experienced hallucinations, illusions, or mental images. In addition, people can be led to think they have seen ghosts by the power of suggestion or the mood created by old-fashioned furnishings. Nickell explains that proprietors of hotels and restaurants sometimes claim that their establishments are haunted—or even create elaborate haunting hoaxes—in order to promote their business. The author concludes that psychics and others who claim to perceive ghosts are most likely just people with fantasy-prone personalities.

Nickell is the senior research fellow at the Committee for the Scientific Explanation of Claims of the Paranormal and the author of many books, including *Camera Clues: A Hand-*

Joe Nickell, "Haunted Inns: Tales of Spectral Ghosts," *Skeptical Inquirer*, September 2000. Copyright © 2000 by The Committee for the Scientific Investigation of Claims of the Paranormal. Reproduced by permission.

*book of Photographic Investigation, Real Life X-Files: Investigating the Paranormal, and Entities: Angels, Spirits, Demons, and Other Alien Beings.*

If testimonials in countless books and articles are to be believed, spending the night in a quaint old hotel might provide an encounter with an extra, ethereal visitor.

Over nearly thirty years of paranormal investigation, I have had the opportunity to experience many "haunted" sites. These have included burial places, like England's West Kennet Long Barrow (where I failed to see the specter of a "Druid priest" that allegedly attends the ancient tomb); religious sanctuaries, such as Christ Church Cathedral in Fredericton, New Brunswick, Canada (where the apparition of the first bishop's wife did not materialize); theaters, including the Lancaster (New York) Opera House (where a ghostly "Lady in Lavender" was a no-show); houses, like the historic residence of William Lyon Mackenzie in Toronto (where ghostly footfalls on the stairs were actually those of real people on a staircase next door); and other sites, notably inns—the subject of this investigative roundup. (Most of the inns cited—all personally investigated—included an overnight stay, staff interviews, background research, etc.)

Why haunted inns? Obviously, places open to the public have more numerous and more varied visitors, and hence more opportunities for ghostly experiences, than do private dwellings and out-of-the-way sites. And inns—by which I include hotels, motels, guesthouses, bed-and-breakfasts, and other places that provide overnight lodging—offer much more. They not only allow extended time periods for visitors to have unusual experiences but also ensure that the guests will be there during a range of states from alertness through sleep. Almost predictably, sooner or later, someone will awaken to an apparition at his or her bedside.

## Hallucinations

The experience is a common type of hallucination, known popularly as a "waking dream," which takes place between being fully asleep and fully awake. Such experiences typically include bizarre imagery (bright lights or apparitions of demons, ghosts, aliens, etc.) and/or auditory hallucinations. "Sleep paralysis" may also occur, whereby there is an inability to move because the body is still in the sleep mode.

A good example of an obvious waking dream is reported by "A.C." She was asleep on board the Queen Mary, the former ocean liner that, since 1971, has been permanently docked at Long Beach, California. As reported by Robert Wlodarski, Anne Nathan-Wlodarski, and Richard Senate in their 1995 book *A Guide to the Haunted Queen Mary*, the woman relates:

> I awoke from a deep sleep around midnight. I saw a figure walking near my daughter's sleeping bag toward the door. Thinking it was my sister, I called out. There was no answer. It was then that I noticed my sister was lying next to me. I sat up in bed and watched the person in white walk through the door!

Another example reported at the Hotel Queen Mary is credited to "H.V.":

> I was awakened from my sleep and observed the image of a person standing in front of my bed. There were no apparent physical features, but it appeared to be holding a flashlight, with a light shining out of it that was brighter than the form itself. I watched as the image swayed back and forth. When I called my roommate the image backed up. I called again and the vision backed up even further, toward the door. I reached for the light switch and tried to turn it on. The light switch seemed to spark and wouldn't turn on all the way. Finally, my roommate woke up; the light came on, and what-

ever it was, was gone. We slept with the TV on the rest of the
night. It was a great experience, and I had a lot of fun!

## A Brief Glimpse

To be sure, not all sightings of ghostly figures are of the
waking-dream variety, many in fact occurring during normal activity. Some are like the report of "J.M." who was at
the Queen Mary's Purser's Desk when, he stated, "I caught a
brief glimpse out of the corner of my eye, of someone or
something moving," or like that of "P.T." who said, "I saw
something move out of the corner of my eye . . . a brief
glimpse of someone or something." Actually, the illusion
that something is moving in the peripheral vision is quite
common. The typical cause may be a "floater," a bit of drift-
ing material in the eye's vitreous humour, although a
twitching eyelid, or other occurrence is also possible.

Such an illusion or a different stimulus—a noise, a subjective feeling, etc.—might trigger, as in one experiencer
aboard the Queen Mary, a mental image. In that case it was
of a man wearing a blue mechanic's uniform—a "feeling"
which left after a few moments. In certain especially imaginative individuals the mental image might be superimposed upon the visual scene, thus creating a seemingly apparitional event.

This may be the explanation for a frequently reported type
of apparition that is seen momentarily and then vanishes
when the percipient looks away for an instant. For example,
a New Mexico hotel, La Posada de Santa Fe—which is allegedly haunted by the spirit of Julie Staab (1844–1896),
wife of the original builder—offers no fewer than three
sightings of this type. One was reported in 1979 by an em-
ployee who was cleaning one night. Although the place was
deserted he looked up to see a translucent woman standing
near a fireplace. Inexplicably, notes Robin Mead, author of

*Haunted Hotels: A Guide to American and Canadian Inns and Their Ghosts,* he "returned to his cleaning," an act that . . . showed "remarkable composure." Then, "when he looked up again the figure had vanished." On another occasion a security guard showed less reserve when, seeing what he thought was Julie, "He turned and ran, and when he looked back, the figure had vanished." Yet again, a "beautifully dressed" Julie, reposing in an armchair, was seen by the hotel phone operator. However, "When she looked back at the chair a few seconds later, the ghost had vanished." Such reports suggest that the apparition is only a mental image that occurs in a kind of reverie.

Indeed, personal experience as well as research data demonstrates that ghostly perceptions often derive from daydreams or other altered states of consciousness. E. Haraldsson for instance specifically determined that apparitional sightings were linked to periods of reverie. As well, Andrew MacKenzie demonstrated that a third of the hallucinatory cases he studied occurred either just before or after sleep, or while the percipient was in a relaxed state or concentrating on some activity like reading, or was performing routine work. The association of apparitional experiences with a dream-like state was also reported by G.N.M. Terrell. He observed that apparitions of people invariably appear fully clothed and are frequently accompanied by objects, just as they are in dreams, because the clothing and other objects are required by the apparitional drama. The three La Posada encounters are consistent with all of these research observations. That the apparitions vanish when the observer's gaze is shifted could be explained by the hypothesis that the reverie is merely broken.

Whereas "waking-dream" type encounters are obviously more likely to be experienced by hotel guests rather than employees, the reverie or daydream type is often reported by the latter—as in all three of the La Posada examples, as well as some of the instances from the Queen Mary and elsewhere. Hotel staff performing routine chores may be particularly susceptible to this type of apparitional experience.

## Suggestion and Mood

The power of suggestion can help trigger ghostly encounters. According to noted psychologist and fellow ghostbuster Robert A. Baker, "We tend to see and hear those things we believe in." Even without the prompting that comes from an inn's reputation for being haunted, the mere ambiance of places with antique architecture and quaint decor can set the stage for spirits to debut. An example is Belhurst Castle, a turreted stone inn in Geneva, New York, whose high-ceilinged lobby is graced with wood paneling, a large fireplace, and a suit of armor to help conjure up romantic notions. Historic sites like Maine's Kennebunk Inn (expanded from a home built in 1799), the Farnsworth House in Gettysburg, Pennsylvania, (constructed in 1810 and its south side pockmarked with bullet holes from the Battle of Gettysburg), and even the more recent Hotel Boulderado in Boulder, Colorado (which opened on New Year's Day 1909 and boasts among its former guests Bat Masterson), offer the impress of history and legend. So does the Bardstown, Kentucky, Jailer's Inn, a bed-and-breakfast converted from the old Nelson County Jail (built in 1819), and, in Santa Fe, the historic adobe La Fonda Inn.

The influence of setting and mood on reports of phantoms is sometimes acknowledged even by those who approach the subject with great credulity, although they may interpret the linkage differently. Broadcaster Andrew Green, for example, in his 1995 treatise *Haunted Inns and Taverns*, says of some copies of English pubs in Europe, the United States, and elsewhere: "A few have reproduced the ambiance so successfully that ghostly manifestations, such as might be associated with a genuine article, have occurred there." Green opines that the "genial atmosphere" of such taverns attracts authentic English ghosts. He seems not to consider the possibility that the setting merely influences the imaginations of those making the reports.

In contrast is the knowing statement of ghost hunter Mason Winfield—referring to the allegedly haunted Holiday Inn at Grand Island, New York—that "The environment of the Inn is not the gloomy, historic sort that puts people in mind of spooks." As one who has spent an uneventful night in that resort hotel, indeed in its reputedly most-haunted room 422, I quite agree. But apparitions can occur anywhere. The Holiday Inn's child ghost "Tanya" apparently originated with an impressionable maid who was cleaning the fourth-floor room shortly after the hotel opened in 1973. The housekeeper suddenly glimpsed a little girl standing in the doorway and, startled, dropped a couple of drinking glasses. When she looked up again, the child was gone. As the maid tried to flee, it was reported, "somehow her cart trapped her in the room. She screamed." Her apparitional encounter seems consistent with the typical conditions we have already discussed: at the time, she was performing routine chores. As to the cart, most likely, flustered, she merely encountered it where she had left it, blocking her flight, and panicked.

Other sightings there—like that of a Canadian man who awoke to see a little girl at the foot of his bed—were of the waking-dream variety. But why is it often a little girl (even if varyingly identified as age "five or six" or "about age 10")? Those knowing about "Tanya" before their sighting may thus be influenced, while those who do not may, in light of subsequent statements or leading questions from those to whom they report an incident, reinterpret a vague sense of presence or a shadowy form as the expected ghost child. To compound the problem, many of the reports are at second- or third-hand, or an even greater remove.

Researching tales like that of the Holiday Inn's child specter can be illuminating. In that case there is no evidence to support claims made by Dennis William Hauck, author of *Haunted Places: The National Directory*, of "a little girl who was burned to death in a house that formerly stood on the site." The Grand Island historian was unable to document any deadly fire at that locale. The only known blaze at the site occurred in 1963, at which time the historic John Nice mansion had been transformed into a restaurant, and there was not a single fatality. My search of the nearby White-haven Cemetery, where the Nice family is buried, failed to turn up any credible candidate for the role of ghost-girl, least of all one named "Tanya"—which, as census and cemetery records show, was not the name of any of John Nice's ten daughters. . . .

## Hoaxes

Ghost tales may indeed be good for business. Explained an owner of one restaurant with bar, which, according to Arthur Myers, author of *The Ghostly Register*, "had a reputation for having ghosts": "It was good conversation for the kind of business we're in. I never tried to dissuade anyone." Other proprietors may go even further. An alleged ghost at the Kennebunk Inn in Kennebunk, Maine, may have originated with the purchase of the inn by one of its earlier owners. He reportedly told a bartender one night that he was "going to make up a story about a ghost," presumably to promote the inn. Years later the former bartender related the story to the current owner, who in turn told me. . . .

Hoaxes do occur. For example, I caught one pranking "ghost" flagrante delecto. In 1999 I accompanied a teacher and ten high school students from Denver's Colorado Academy on an overnight stay in a "haunted" hotel. Located in the Rocky Mountains, in the old mining town of Fairplay (where an art teacher conducts "ghost tours"), the Hand Hotel was built in 1931. In the early evening as we gathered in the lobby beneath mounted elk heads and bear skins, the lights of the chandelier flickered mysteriously. But the teacher and I both spied the surreptitious action of the desk clerk, whose sheepish smile acknowledged that one brief hotel mystery had been solved.

Other signs of pranking there included a "ghost" photo (displayed in a lobby album) that the clerk confided to me was staged, and some pennies, placed on the back of a men's room toilet, that from time to time would secretly become rearranged to form messages—like the word "why?" that I encountered. This obvious running prank invited other mischief makers (like one student) to join in.

## Professional Psychics

Ghostly presences are hyped at many inns when "psychics" visit the premises. One session at the Farnsworth House was part of a television production for Halloween, an indication of how much credibility should be afforded it. Brookdale Lodge, near Santa Cruz, California (which I investigated for a Discovery Channel documentary that aired May 24, 1998), once invited Sylvia Browne. A regular on the *Montel Williams* TV show, the self-claimed clairvoyant and medium envisioned a ghost girl that she named "Sara," helping to bring the total number of entities thus far "detected" at Brookdale to forty-nine—and counting. Such psychics typically offer unsubstantiated, even unverifiable claims, or information that is already known. This may be gleaned in advance from research sources or obtained by the "psychic" from persons who have such knowledge through the technique of "cold reading" (an artful method of fishing for information employed by shrewd fortunetellers). Alternatively, the psychic may make numerous pronouncements, trusting that others will count the apparent hits and ignore, or interpret appropriately, the misses.

This is not to say that all such pronouncements are insincere. Those who fancy themselves psychics may exhibit the traits associated with a "fantasy-prone" personality. That is a designation for an otherwise normal person with an unusual ability to fantasize. As a child, he or she may have an imaginary playmate and live much of the time in make-believe worlds. As an adult, the person continues to spend much time fantasizing, and may report apparitional, out-of-body, or near-death experiences; claim psychic or healing powers; receive special messages from higher beings; be easily hypnotized; and/or exhibit other traits. Anyone may have some of these traits, but fantasizers have them in profusion. Sylvia Browne, for example, as a child had what her parents called "made-up friends," particularly a "spirit guide"—still with her—that she named "Francine." Browne undergoes "trances" in which "Francine" provides alleged information from "Akashic records, individual spirit guides, and messages from the Godhead." Browne also claims to see apparitions, talk to ghosts, have clairvoyant visions, make psychic medical diagnoses, divine past lives, etc. She has even started her own religion, Novus Spiritus ("New Spirit").

The use of psychics is a stock in trade of many so-called parapsychologists. Among them is Hans Holzer, one of whose many books bills him as "the world's leading expert on haunted houses" while another avows that his "cases" were "carefully investigated under scientifically stringent conditions." Unfortunately, these claims are belied by Holzer's credulous acceptance of "spirit" photos, anecdotal reports, and other doubtful evidence. For example, he "investigated" a former stagecoach inn at Thousand Oaks, California, by relying on self-styled "witch" Sybil Leek (1922–1982). In one room Leek "complained of being cold all over" and "felt" that a man had been murdered there. No verification was provided and Holzer admits she "did not connect with a female ghost whose 'presence' had been 'sensed'" by the inn's owners. Nevertheless Holzer casually opines that "Like inns in general, this one may have more undiscovered ghosts hanging on the spot."

Professional psychics like Sybil Leek and Sylvia Browne aside, we may wonder whether ordinary "ghost" percipients also have similar tendencies toward fantasizing. Over nearly three decades of ghost investigating I have noticed a pattern. In interviewing residents or staff of an allegedly haunted site, I would usually find a few who had no ghostly experiences—for example a bell captain at La Fonda Inn in Santa Fe who had spent forty-three years there. Others might have moderate experiences—like hearing a strange noise or witnessing some unexplained physical occurrence such as a door mysteriously opening—that they attributed to a ghost. Often, those interviewed would direct me to one or more persons whom they indicated had had intensive haunting encounters, including seeing apparitions, in short, I usually found a spectrum that ranged from outright skepticism to mediumistic experiences. I also sensed a difference in the people: some appeared down-to-earth and level-headed, while others—I thought—seemed more imaginative and impulsive, recounting with dramatic flair their phantomesque adventures. I had no immediate way of objectively measuring what I thought I was observing, but I gave it much thought.

At length I developed a questionnaire that, on the one hand, measures the number and intensity of ghostly experiences, and, on the other, counts the number of exhibited traits associated with fantasy-proneness. Tabulation of a limited number of questionnaires administered thus far shows a strong correlation between these two areas—that, as the level of haunting experiences rises, the fantasy scale tends to show a similarly high score.

As this and other evidence indicates, to date there is no credible scientific evidence that inns—or any other sites—are inhabited by spirits of the dead. As Robert A. Baker often remarks, "There are no haunted places, only haunted people."

# "Ghost Photos" Do Not Prove That Houses Are Haunted

Robert Novella

Since the mid–nineteenth century, when photography was invented, people have made claims about photographs purporting to show ghosts or evidence of ghosts. In the early days, the image of a second person—the ghost—would often show up in a portrait of someone else. Other photos showed mediums exuding ectoplasm (a filmy substance said to be the matter that allows ghosts to be seen) from their mouths or other parts of their body. Looking at those photos today, most of them are clearly fakes or accidents such as a double exposure.

Today's sophisticated photography equipment makes it possible to fake very convincing ghosts, but even more convincing to many people than high-tech frauds are the

Robert Novella, "Photographic Fakery," *New England Journal of Skepticism,* vol. 1, Winter 1998. Copyright © 1998 by *New England Journal of Skepticism.* Reproduced by permission.

"ghosts" ordinary people capture with ordinary cameras. These include "orbs" (small or large white transparent circles), spiraling ghostly "worms" or "rods," foggy patches, and even ectoplasm-like images that show up unexpectedly in photo prints even though the photographer saw nothing unusual when he or she shot the photo.

While these photographic phenomena serve as evidence of ghosts to some people, others, like Robert Novella, the author of the following viewpoint, say they can be explained by simply understanding the photography process. In this selection he describes some of the photographic accidents that can cause "ghost photos." Novella is a founder of the New England Skeptics Society.

Tales of ghosts and spirits can be quite compelling and convincing but many people view photographs of these ghostly phenomena as better evidence or even proof of their existence. They have been proffered as evidence ever since the development of modern photography in 1839. Images generally range from bright spots of light and wispy smoke-like forms to detailed images of human faces. But, disregarding hoaxes, many convincing photographs can more easily be explained as photographic artifacts produced accidentally by the photographer, the developer, or even the camera manufacturer.

## "Ghosts"—Photographic Artifacts

Photographic artifacts are anomalous images in photos caused by poor camera work, faulty camera design or improper developing. They are ubiquitous because millions of people take photographs every day throughout the world and because cameras are readily available and inexpensive.

Once there are enough people involved in an activity, any activity, even rare events become more and more commonplace. Exacerbating this is the fact that most of these photographers are non-professionals with little technical knowledge and experience in proper camera work. The result is a glut of poor pictures with unusual images that seem to defy conventional explanation. Since many people are enamored with the paranormal and rarely, if ever, consider more mundane explanations for mysterious phenomena, a metaphysical conclusion is quickly and easily reached. What they do not realize is that these more mundane explanations concerning artifacts are the simplest explanations and they have been shown to be responsible for all "ghost" photographs that have been seriously investigated. The principle of parsimony (Occam's Razor) guides us in these situations, recommending that the simplest explanation, among two or more that explain the same phenomena equally well, should be ruled out before more complex ones are supported. There are many types of photographic artifacts but they can be distilled down to five major types; flashback, multiple exposure, light diffraction, camera cords, and light leakage.

## Flashback Causes Ghostly Forms

Flashback, probably the most common artifact found in photographs, is caused by excessive reflected light from the camera's flash which overexposes part of the film causing a glare spot or "washed out" area. Typically, the image looks like a bright undefined form on the film, or a white patch. To determine if a flash was used, simply look for sharp shadows and a brightly lit foreground. Ed and Lorraine Warren, Connecticut's famous Ghostbusters, have a website in which they discussed ways to produce pictures of real ghosts. In it they recommend using a flash, the brighter the better. Even they were unsure why this should be a factor considering their belief that spirits often impress the images themselves onto the film. However, there is no discussion or any recognition at all that the light images might be the result of photographic artifact created by the flash.

## Multiple Exposures Create "Apparitions"

Double or multiple exposures can also produce mystifying images that are easily misinterpreted. If two pictures are taken without advancing the film, the resulting photograph will show both images in the same photograph. Because there are multiple images superimposed over each other, a very eerie effect is produced resulting in images that seem to be transparent and ghostlike. This is relatively easy to do on purpose but can also be accomplished accidentally with cheaply made cameras or a lack of camera knowledge. If the film is not loaded properly the film may not advance as it should, thereby exposing two or more images onto the same frame of the negative. Even if the film is correctly loaded, the frame advance mechanism could malfunction, not an uncommon occurrence with inexpensive cameras. To reproduce this yourself simply photograph a solitarily lit subject, then rewind the camera film and take another picture. Some cameras even have a special setting that is specifically designed for multiple exposure. If this is done with care, very convincing photos can be produced that seem to cry out for a paranormal explanation, unless, of course, you are familiar with artifacts.

## Vortices and Ghost Rods

Paranormal investigator Joe Nickell made a valuable contribution to the field of photographic artifact when he discovered, through experimentation and common sense, the camera cord effect (Nickell 96). Camera cords might seem quite unrelated to ghosts but I believe they are responsible for a host of ghost photographs in which a blurry loop or strand-like image appears. They have been variously called "ghost rods", "dimensional doorways" or "vortices" by true believers, but most likely they are just another type of photographic artifact caused by subcompact cameras. Subcompacts, like other non-reflex cameras, have direct vision viewfinders which have separate apertures for viewing subjects and for the lens. In contrast, SLR (single lens reflex) cameras use an angled mirror behind the lens that redirects the light from the lens to the photographer's eye, (35 millimeter SLRs use a series of silvered surfaces inside a pentaprism to achieve this effect). The result is that non-SLR cameras provide a view for the eye that is slightly different from what would otherwise be seen through the lens. Therefore if there is an object close to the lens it will not be noticed, increasing the chance of producing this artifact. If the cord drops in front of the camera it cannot be seen, resulting in a whitish blurry image of a curving strand-like object. If it is closer to the lens it will produce a more diffuse, mist-like effect. The cord does not appear black, its typical color, because it is brightly reflecting the light from the flash only inches away. Camera cords are not required for the camera cord effect, however; any object will suffice, be it a thumb, hair, jewelry, or even clothing. Any time direct vision viewfinders are used, one must guard against, but not be surprised if, ghost rods make an appearance.

## Balls of Light and Orbs

Sometimes artifacts reveal themselves as balls of light, often referred to as ghost globules [or orbs]. Many people believe that these globules are a form of spirit energy that has chosen to manifest itself as glowing spheres. As you might expect, this is not the only possible explanation. These images are curiously reminiscent of two phenomena; light diffraction and lens flares. The former occurs when light waves, moving from one medium to another (such as from air into a water droplet), change direction and interact with one another producing light and dark regions (depending on whether there is constructive or destructive interference). This can happen when a photograph is taken if there is condensation on the lens or particles in the air. As one anomalous image expert noted, "If you take a photograph by night using a flashlight, tiny particles of dust or raindrops in front of the camera may appear on the picture like brilliant balls of light" (Mosbleck). Lens flares produce this effect when the camera is pointed towards or near a bright light source which scatters the light among the various lens elements. These inter-reflections produce images of the lens elements in a straight line moving away from the light source. Both diffraction and lens flares, being simpler explanations, should be ruled out before advocating the existence of something extraordinary and unverified like ghost globules. This is what good scientists do and it is what the scientific method demands.

## The Golden Door

Some artifacts are not only unique to certain classes of cameras but also to a specific brand within a class. The Polaroid One Step, for example, has been shown to produce a unique anomaly called "The Golden Door." When this camera is pointed at a bright source of light, the developed photograph shows a rectangular shape surrounded by a halo of golden light. This has been taken to signify the doorway to heaven mentioned in Revelation 4:1. One does not need to refer to the Bible to understand this, however. Through experimentation and trial and error, Georgia skeptic Dale Heatherington discovered that he was able to reliably reproduce this effect with the One Step camera. Further examination revealed that the door-like shape and halo of light was caused by light reflecting off the iris or aperture of the camera.

## Angel Wings

Light leakage or fogging is yet another phenomenon that can wreak havoc with your pictures. Light can leak onto the film at any point from its loading to development causing unusual and unique patterns that are especially reminiscent of ghosts. This non-image forming light typically reaches the film if the back of the camera is opened prematurely, if the door is ill fitting or loose, or if the camera is loaded in a brightly lit area. An artifact common to Polaroids called "Angel Wings" is an example of light leakage in which a fan shaped image of light has leaked onto the negative. The term "fogging" also includes, more specifically, artifacts created by x-rays, heat and stress on the negative or photo paper itself. Airport x-rays, a hot car, or rough handling of the film can all cause fogging. To determine if any of this has happened to your film, simply look for the anomaly on the film negative. If it extends beyond the frame of the picture then you have been fogged. I've examined hundreds of ghost photos on the web, and this artifact is well represented, if incorrectly interpreted.

## Unseen by the Human Eye

It is very significant that in the vast majority of cases, nothing unusual is noticed when a ghost photograph is taken. It is extremely rare to hear someone say that they saw a ghost and then grabbed a camera to take a picture of it. Most often the spirit or ghost rod is not discovered until the photographs return from the developers. This should serve as a strong indication that the image is an artifact of the photographic process and not something that was actually there.

Some believers respond to this by saying that the film is picking up light that the human eye cannot perceive. Actually, the majority of modern film is designed to react primarily to the visible portion of the electromagnetic spectrum, just like the human eye. There is some sensitivity to ultraviolet, but manufacturers try to minimize this by adding dyes to the emulsion and adding special coatings to the lens. What little UV light that might reach the film would have a bluish cast to it, not the ubiquitous whitish shapes found in most ghost photos.

It is important to note that the artifacts discussed above are only the most common and best documented artifactual phenomena. There are many other types of artifacts, each producing different types of images in different situations. Light interaction within a camera is a very complex phenomena that few photographers take the time to appreciate. For this reason, anytime an anomalous image appears that does not seem amenable to the descriptions I have offered above, it does not mean that you have a genuine ghost photo. Such a conclusion would not be justified. What is required is a rational investigation by people knowledgeable about photography and the behavior of light and not rash conclusions based on appeal and desire and little else.

## References

P. DeAngelis & S. Novella, "Hunting the Ghost Hunters," *The Connecticut Skeptic*, vol. 2, issue 3.

Hedgecoe, John. *John Hedgecoe's New Book of Photography*, DK Publishing Inc., N.Y.

Mosbleck, *The Elusive Photographic Evidence*, 208 (quote references UFO photographs).

Nickell, Joe, 1994. *Camera Clues: A Handbook for Photographic Investigation*, Lexington: University Press of Kentucky.

———, "Ghostly Photos," *Skeptical Inquirer*, vol. 20, no. 4, 1996, pp. 13–14.

# Epilogue: Analyzing the Evidence

When considering a controversial topic like haunted houses, it is important to carefully look at the available evidence from more than one point of view. You can begin to shape your beliefs by critically examining the evidence provided by experts who have studied the topic of haunted houses and the evidence from those who claim to have experienced a haunted house. Each article in this book provides various kinds of evidence and makes various kinds of arguments favoring or challenging the reality of haunted houses. Some articles directly contradict others. It is your job to decide which articles present a truthful and reasonable case.

You can do this by reading each article critically. This does not mean that you criticize, or say negative things about, an article. It means that you analyze and evaluate what the author says. This chapter describes a critical reading technique and practices using it to evaluate the articles in this book. You can use the same technique to evaluate information about other topics.

## The Author

In deciding whether an article provides good evidence for or against the existence of haunted houses, it can be helpful to find out something about the author. Consider whether the author has any special qualifications for writing about the subject. For example, in this book some authors describe their personal experiences of living in a haunted house. Others have credentials as investigators or scientists. You will have to decide what kind of experience makes an author more credible.

In this book, the editor has provided at least a small amount of information about each author. Use this information to start forming your opinion about the author's claims.

## Hypothetical Reasoning

Despite whether you know anything about the author, you can evaluate an article on its own merits by using hypothetical reasoning. This is a method for determining whether an author has made a reasonable case for his or her claims. For example, Hanz Holzer, author of the article "A Psychic's Visit Proves that San Diego's Whaley House Is Haunted," claims that the psychic who accompanied him on his investigation had contact with ghosts. You can use hypothetical reasoning to decide whether he has made a reasonable case supporting this claim. (Keep in mind that hypothetical reasoning will not necessarily prove that an author's claims are true—only that he or she has made a reasonable case for the claims. By determining this, you know whether the arguments are worth considering.)

To use hypothetical reasoning to analyze an article, you will use five steps:

- State the author's claim (the hypothesis).
- Gather the author's evidence supporting the claim.
- Examine the author's evidence.
- Consider alternative hypotheses, or explanations, for the evidence.
- Draw a conclusion about the author's claim.

Using hypothetical reasoning to examine several articles on haunted houses can give you a better perspective on the topic. You will begin to discern the difference between strong and weak evidence and to see which point of view has the most—or the best—evidence supporting it.

The following sections show how to use hypothetical reasoning to critically examine some of the articles in this book. You can practice applying the method to other articles.

## 1. State the Author's Claim

A hypothesis is a factual statement that can be tested to determine the likelihood of its truth. In other words, it is not merely someone's opinion; by testing it, you can find out if it is likely to be true or false. To evaluate an article critically, start by stating the author's claim. This will be the hypothesis you are going to test as you critically examine the article. Be aware than an author may make several claims. To simplify, the following table states only one claim for each article.

One important thing to remember when you write a hypothesis is that it should be a factual statement that is clear, specific, and provable. For example, the first hypothesis stated in the table, "Certain signs prove a house is haunted," is vague. A better, more specific hypothesis would be, "Apparitions of dead people are one sign that a house is haunted."

Be aware that not every article has a provable hypothesis. If an article is purely a writer's opinion, you may not be able to state a provable hypothesis. Likewise, some authors avoid stating any clear claim. For example, many newspaper and magazine article writers attempt to remain as objective as possible about a topic. They simply report what happened and what people said about it. You may not be able to write a provable hypothesis for such an article.

In the table below, several hypothesis spaces have been left empty. Write a clear, specific, and provable hypothesis for each of these articles.

| Author | Hypothesis |
|---|---|
| Patricia Telesco | Certain signs prove a house is haunted. |

| Author | Hypothesis |
|---|---|
| Harry Price | Borley Rectory is haunted. |
| Hanz Holzer | |
| Ed and Lorraine Warren with Robert David Chase | The Amityville House is haunted. |
| Peter Carter | Proper use of feng shui may rid a house of ghosts. |
| Randolph W. Liebeck | An investigator can use measuring tools to determine if a house is haunted. |
| Margaret Mittlebach and Michael Crewdson | |
| Eric J. Dingwall, Kathleen M. Goldney, and Trevor H. Hall | Harry Price faked the Borley Rectory hauntings. |
| Joe Nickell with John F. Fischer | The MacKenzie House haunting can be explained by normal physical phenomena. |
| Loyd Auerbach | |
| Joe Nickell | |
| Robert Novella | |

## 2. Gather the Author's Evidence Supporting the Claim

Once you have a hypothesis, you must gather the evidence the author uses to support that hypothesis. The evidence is everything the author uses to prove that his or her claim is true. Sometimes an individual sentence is a piece of evidence. Sometimes a string of paragraphs or a section of the article is a piece of evidence. Let's look at the article by Harry Price, "Borley Rectory Was the Most Haunted House in England." Here is some of Price's evidence:

    1. A respectable London newspaper reported on the rectory's haunting.

2. Price asserts that Borley Rectory is "the most haunted house in England."
3. The house's haunted past is well documented.
4. Many people have reported seeing a ghostly horse-drawn coach "careering through the grounds" and many other apparitions.
5. Mr. Robinson, one of the house's residents at the time this article was written, told of many odd incidents, including a loud doorbell ringing on its own account, door keys falling out of locks, the sounds of slippered footfalls, mysteriously thrown stones, and lights in empty rooms.
6. Price interviewed other people who also gave accounts of ghostly incidents.
7. Price and his secretary thoroughly investigated the wiring of the doorbell and other parts of the house and could find nothing that suggested a hoax.
8. Price and a reporter witnessed a ghostly figure on the lawn.
9. Price saw a pane of glass mysteriously fall to the ground, narrowly missing him and the reporter, and a glass candlestick hurled at him by an unseen force.
10. Price and others conducted a séance during which something rapped out answers to questions.
11. After Price's visit, Mr. Robinson reported that someone or something unknown had unlocked and opened the windows from inside the house.

## 3. Examine the Evidence the Author Uses to Support the Claim

An author might use many types of evidence to support his or her claims. It is important to recognize different types of evidence and to evaluate whether they actually support the author's claims. In this article, Price relies most heavily on eyewitness testimony (items 4, 5, 6, 8, 9, 10, and 11). He also relies on expert or celebrity testimonials (item 1), physical evidence—or lack of it—(items 7 and 9), and statements of fact (item 3) and opinion (item 2).

*Eyewitness testimony* (items 4, 5, 6, 8, 9, 10, and 11). For some people, eyewitness accounts alone are enough to convince them that haunted houses are genuine. However, a scientist would examine such accounts carefully because eyewitness testimony is notoriously unreliable.

Perhaps you know about the eyewitness experiment in which a group of people is sitting in a classroom listening to a lecture or doing some other activity. Suddenly, the classroom door bursts open, and a stranger enters. The stranger may "rob" one of the witnesses or do something else dramatic. Then the stranger leaves.

A few moments later, the instructor asks the students to tell what they witnessed. Invariably, different students remember different things. One remembers that the stranger was of average height and weight; another remembers that he was thin or heavy. One remembers that he had red hair; another remembers that a hood covered the stranger's head. One remembers that he was carrying a weapon; another remembers that his hands were empty.

There are a lot of reasons for these different recollections. When something unexpected occurs, especially when it happens quickly or when it evinces great emotion, the mind is not prepared to remember details. Even when the event is expected, witnesses may remember things differently because they are not good observers. Or the witnesses may have preconceived ideas that influence their observations; for example, they may believe that robbers are male, so when they see a robber whose features are not clear, they assume the person must be male. Sometimes witnesses have recently experienced something that influences what they see; for example, a person who has just come home from a scary movie and hears an unusual sound in the house may feel certain he or she is about to be set upon by a monster or a serial killer. In the case Price describes, a long tradition held that the house was haunted, so people living in it or visiting it might be inclined to attribute unusual events to ghosts.

For all these reasons and more, a reader has to be careful about accepting eyewitness testimony as the main source of evidence. In crime investigations, the police often try to find independent corroborating witnesses—several people who saw the same event and have not spoken with each other so that their accounts have not been influenced by anyone else's version. If two or more witnesses independently report the same details, the chances are better that the details are accurate. In this case, Price and a reporter together witnessed a phantom figure. Your job as a critical reader is to decide whether Price's account of this incident is credible. Did he examine the situation carefully enough to conclude that it was indeed a ghost they saw?

*Expert or celebrity testimonials* (item 1). Many writers support their hypotheses with testimony from a celebrity or an expert. An easy way to understand the use of celebrity or expert testimonial is to look at television ads. A lot of them use this persuasive technique. For example, you have probably seen pop stars and famous athletes in commercials selling cars, shoes, cell phones, and food products, and you likely have seen medicine commercials in which doctors describe the benefits of a product. Advertisers know that many people are influenced when a celebrity or expert says something is true. Article writers know this as well.

Keep in mind that celebrity testimony usually does not have much value as evidence: If a celebrity likes a certain brand of shoes, does it mean the shoes are comfortable and will wear well? Not necessarily. What it really means is that the celebrity's agent got the celebrity a certain amount of money to say the shoes are good.

However, some expert testimony can serve as valuable evidence. For example, in an article about car safety, a scientist who conducts experimental car crashes for the U.S. government can probably provide some valuable information. (But the testimony of the government car-crash expert will probably not be helpful if the author is writing about haunted houses unless the expert has some kind of valid experience with that topic as well.)

The key to evaluating testimonial evidence is determining whether the celebrity or expert is knowledgeable about the topic under consideration. The author must provide enough background so that the reader can judge whether the celebrity or expert is qualified to provide valuable information.

In this article, Harry Price uses a form of expert testimonial. The London newspaper that reported on Borley Rectory is a well-known, respected publication. Price hopes that the newspaper's reputation will convince the reader that the alleged hauntings of this house are worth considering seriously.

*Physical evidence* (items 7 and 9). Physical evidence can be used to prove or disprove a hypothesis. In police cases, physical evidence includes fingerprints, DNA, and murder weapons. Ghost cases do not often turn up much physical evidence, although some ghost investigators claim their investigative instruments find evidence in the form of changed atmospheric conditions, photographs, recordings, and other unusual clues. In the Price article, the physical evidence is more accurately called negative evidence. Price and his secretary looked for possible physical explanations for phenomena such as the doorbell mysteriously ringing, but they found nothing. For example, all the electrical wiring appeared to be completely normal. If the reader accepts Mr. Robinson's report in item 11, that report could also be considered physical evidence. The windows had been sealed, but something unknown opened them. If no signs of tampering were found, that would be a form of negative physical evidence. (If fingerprints, pry marks, or other such clues were found, they would be physical evidence that it was not a ghost that opened the windows.)

It is important to note that negative physical evidence is generally not considered nearly as important as positive evidence. Just because a fingerprint has not been found does not prove that no one touched a windowsill; it could mean that the fingerprints were wiped away or that the person who opened the window wore gloves.

*Statements of fact* (items 1 and 3). A statement of fact presents verifiable information—that is, it can be proven to be true or false. Either the author verifies the information by providing the source of the information or the reader researches and determines whether the statement is true. Ideally, the author should tell the source of any statement of fact so that the reader can confirm it. But many authors simply expect the reader to take their word for it. Be careful about accepting facts just because an author states them.

In this case, it might be difficult to find out how thoroughly Price and his secretary investigated the house. Basically, the reader has to decide whether to accept Price's word on this, probably based on the kind of detail he provides. Then the reader must decide how important these statements of fact are in proving that the house is haunted. For example, does a long history of people believing a place is haunted make it so?

*Statements of opinion* (item 2). A statement of opinion cannot be proven true or false—it is simply what someone believes. (Statements of opinion often are based on or contain factual statements that can be verified. For example, "I think you are angry" is a statement of opinion, but it can be verified when your face turns red and you hit me in the nose.) Whether we accept a statement of opinion as good supporting evidence depends on the nature of the opinion and what we think of the person giving it. For example, if our history teacher says, "Peace in the Middle East will not happen for a very long time," we may accept that as supporting evidence because we respect that teacher's knowledge about world events. But if the same teacher tells us, "Fashion models will be wearing white socks with their black trousers next year," we may be less inclined to take this opinion seriously unless he or she clearly keeps up with the latest fashion trends.

If an author relies heavily on opinion, you will have to decide if the author—or his sources—are reliable. In this case, Harry Price had extensive experience investigating hauntings and other paranormal phenomena, so his background provides credibility. However, his reputation for honest investigation did come under attack, especially after his death. What do you think—does Harry Price's opinion help convince you that Borley Rectory was the most haunted house in England?

## 4. Consider Alternative Hypotheses
Once you have examined the types of evidence the author has provided and considered how valuable the evidence is in supporting the author's claims, notice whether the author has considered other possible explanations. If the author considers only one explanation for the evidence, he or she may be presenting a biased, or one-sided, view or may not have fully considered the issue. Does it seem to you that Harry Price has seriously considered any explanation for the strange goings-on at Borley Rectory besides ghosts?

# 5. Draw a Conclusion About the Author's Claim

After considering the evidence and alternative explanations, it is time to make a judgment, to decide whether the hypothesis makes sense. You can tally up the evidence that does and does not support the hypothesis and see how many pros and cons you have. But that is really too simple. You will have to give more weight to some pieces of evidence than to others. What do you think is Price's most convincing evidence? Is it sufficiently convincing that you agree that Borley Rectory must be haunted?

## Exploring Further

Let's examine another article using hypothetical reasoning. Take a look at Loyd Auerbach's article, "The Amityville 'Haunting' Was a Hoax." Perhaps the first thing to notice is that Auerbach comes to the subject of haunted houses with a bias about it. He is a parapsychologist who writes for *FATE* magazine (a pro-paranormal publication), and some of his investigations have concluded that a haunting was genuine. The fact that he may have a bias in favor of ghosts might lead the reader to conclude that when he says a haunted house is a fake, it probably is. Still, a reader must read carefully and try to determine if Auerbach is presenting an unbiased view of the alleged Amityville haunting.

Now let's review Auerbach's article using the steps for hypothetical reasoning.

*1. State a Hypothesis.* In this case, the title of the article clearly states a hypothesis: The Amityville haunting was a hoax.

*2. Gather the Author's Evidence.* Here is some of Auerbach's evidence:

1. He says that an important witness, Ron DeFeo's attorney, "changed his tune" and said the "haunting"

was a hoax dreamed up by the house's residents (the Lutz family) and himself to gain fame and fortune. This is stated again later in the article by parapsychological investigator Jerry Solfvin.

2. He says that Robert Morris, a skeptical investigator, found several factual discrepancies in the details in the Amityville account. For example, key weather conditions were reported inaccurately.

3. He cites an article in the *Washington Post* that detailed further important factual errors, including the location of the house not actually being on the site of an old Indian refuge for the sick and dying.

4. He points out that the author of the book *The Amityville Horror* had no firsthand knowledge of the supposedly haunted house and never visited it himself.

5. He says that the skeptical parapsychologists the author of *The Amityville Horror* said investigated the house did not; no one investigated until after the residents had moved out. In fact, the parapsychologists told Auerbach that they had not found the case interesting enough to investigate.

6. Alex Tanous and Karlis Osis, among other pro-paranormal investigators, told Auerbach that they believed the haunting was a hoax.

7. These investigators saw a contract for a book or movie when they interviewed the Lutzes after their move from the house.

8. Jerry Solfvin, a pro-paranormal investigator, told Auerbach that when he visited the supposedly haunted house, "it was like a zoo," with television camera crews, *National Enquirer* reporters, sensational demonologists Ed and Lorraine Warren, and others "zooming around the house," saying things like "I see it! I feel it!"

9. Auerbach says this case was a poor one to investigate because the residents quickly moved out of the house and no ghostly events were occurring there by the time investigators became involved.

10. He says the Lutzes' testimony was suspect because it was too extreme and had no objective evidence to support it.

11. He says that the media's involvement encouraged the Lutzes to "get carried away" because the media wants something "flashy" to report, and people greedily give it to them.

12. He says that real people do not have experiences like the extreme ones reported in the Amityville case.

3. *Examine the Evidence.* In his article, Auerbach uses statements of fact (items 1, 2, 3, 4, and 5), statements of opinion (item 11), and expert testimony (items 6, 9, 10, and 12), and he casts aspersions or "tars with the same brush" (items 7 and 8).

*Statements of fact* (items 1, 2, 3, 4, and 5). Review the information on statements of fact. Notice that Auerbach does tell the general sources of his facts, but that without detailed footnotes, you would have to do some time-consuming research to find the actual *Washington Post* article he mentions. Do these facts provide good support for Auerbach's hypothesis?

*Statements of opinion* (items 11 and 12). Review the information on statements of opinion. Do you find these opinions credible? Why?

*Expert testimony* (items 6, 9, 10, and 12). Writers who are researchers, investigators, and scholars tend to cite a lot of experts who can help bolster their case. It is sometimes helpful to look up the original information to find out more about what the cited expert says about the topic. Some authors do not provide source information; they simply name the expert. However, most serious researchers, investigators, and scholars provide full source information in footnotes or a text note so that the original source can easily be found. In this case, Auerbach reports what experts told him personally.

Note that in this article one of the primary experts that Auerbach relies on is himself. He has been investigating haunted houses and other paranormal events for many years. Many authors rely on their own expertise when they present their arguments. One reason we read certain articles is because of the author's expertise.

*Casting aspersions or "tarring with the same brush"* (items 7 and 8). This practice sometimes includes name-calling or ridicule. It involves ways of belittling an opponent or opposing view to reduce its credibility. In item 7, for example, by saying the atmosphere at the Amityville house was "like a zoo," Alex Tanous wants Auerbach and others to believe that no credible investigation could have gone on in such an atmosphere.

"Tarring with the same brush" puts the opponent in the same context as something that the reader already has a low opinion of. Most people consider the *National Enquirer* a scandal sheet with no credibility as a serious publication, so by noting that *National Enquirer* reporters were present, Tanous provides further reason to not take the investigation of the house seriously.

Many times, an author casts aspersions as a substitute for real evidence. You must read carefully to see if any real evidence is present. Do Tanous's statements seem to offer good support for Auerbach's hypothesis?

4. Consider Alternative Hypotheses. Does Auerbach consider alternatives to his hypothesis that the Amityville haunting is a hoax? Can you think of any he should have considered?

5. *Draw a Conclusion About the Author's Claim.* Does Auerbach make a good case for his hypothesis? What evidence most influences your decision?

## Other Kinds of Evidence

Writers use many kinds of evidence in addition to those described above to support their hypotheses. The following are some common examples:

*Anecdotal evidence.* An anecdote is a brief story. Eyewitness testimony, described above, is one type of anecdotal evidence. A legend or traditional story that is related to the topic under discussion is another. Authors use anecdotes to illustrate a point or make an analogy.

Anecdotal evidence contrasts with hard evidence (including facts, physical evidence, and statistical evidence), which investigators usually consider more significant than anecdotal evidence because it is easier to prove or disprove. However, anecdotal evidence can sometimes be strong, especially when multiple witnesses report the same thing.

*Statistical or numerical evidence.* Statistical data can be important in determining the significance of an event. For example, certain haunting symptoms recurring in the same part of a building or at the same time of day again and again may lend more credibility to its truthfulness. Authors also sometimes use numbers to show that a large number of people believe something or have experienced something. They expect that providing high numbers will convince some readers that a hypothesis is true. Evaluate all numerical claims carefully. Where did the numbers come from? If they are from a survey, how old is the survey? What do the numbers really mean?

*Logical reasoning.* Authors often use examples of logical reasoning to lead the reader to the author's desired conclusion. Here is an example: A consumer publication has reported that a certain car gets more miles per gallon than any other popular car on the road. In addition, it has a low repair rate and a low purchase price. Therefore, it is probably a good buy. This seems pretty logical. The danger is that sometimes what seems logical really is not. This is a logical fallacy. Here's an example: I have never seen a ghost; therefore, ghosts do not exist. This is a fallacy because it is an overgeneralization. There are a lot of things you have not experienced that are real. For example, you have not experienced spaceflight, the bubonic plague, or death, yet all exist.

Another kind of logical fallacy is a false analogy—you wrongly compare two things based on a common quality. Here is an example: Dogs wag their tails when they are happy; cats that wag their tails must be happy, too. The fallacy is assuming that cats have the same behavior as dogs even though they are different species. A cat wagging its tail may be angry, indecisive, or ready to pounce on prey. Cats do not typically wag their tails when they are happy.

Sometimes an author does not spell out the logical reasoning. He or she provides part of the reasoning and leaves the reader to assume the rest. This is called implied logical reasoning. For example, the author may write that a man named Dave Parran used to sit in a rocking chair on his porch. Now Dave Parran is dead, and people have reported seeing a transparent figure that appears to be rocking on the porch. The author may not tell you that people are seeing a ghost, but he or she wants you to jump to that conclusion.

Just as with fully spelled-out logical reasoning, if an author uses implied logical reasoning, the reader must decide whether it makes sense.

## Now You Do It!

Choose one article from this book that has not already been analyzed and use hypothetical reasoning to determine if the author's evidence supports the hypothesis. Here is a form you can use:

Name of article_____ Author_____

1. State the author's hypothesis.

2. List the evidence.

3. Examine the evidence. For each item you have listed under number 2, state what type of evidence it is (statement of fact, eyewitness testimony, etc.) and evaluate it: Does it appear to be valid evidence? Does it lend strong support to the author's hypothesis?

4. Consider alternative hypotheses. What alternative hypotheses does the author consider? Does he or she consider them fairly? If the author rejects them, does the rejection seem reasonable? Are there alternative explanations you believe should be considered? Explain.

5. Draw a conclusion about the hypothesis. Does the author adequately support his or her claim? Do you believe the author's hypothesis is credible? Explain.

# For Further Research

## Books About Ghosts

Hazel M. Denning, *True Hauntings: Spirits with a Purpose.* St. Paul, MN: Llewellyn, 1996.

Editors of Time-Life Books, *Phantom Encounters.* Alexandria, VA: Time-Life Books, 1988.

Hilary Evans and Patrick Huyghe, *The Field Guide to Ghosts and Other Apparitions.* New York: Quill/HarperCollins, 2000.

Rosemary Ellen Guiley, *The Encyclopedia of Ghosts and Spirits.* 2nd ed. New York: Facts On File, 2000.

Joe Nickell, *Real-Life X-Files: Investigating the Paranormal.* Lexington: University of Kentucky Press, 2001. *See also other books by this author.*

Tom Ogden, *The Complete Idiot's Guide to Ghosts and Hauntings.* Indianapolis: Macmillan/Alpha Books, 1999.

Harry Price, *Poltergeist: Tales of the Supernatural.* 1945. Reprint, London: Bracken Books, 1993.

William G. Roll, *The Poltergeist.* Metuchen, NJ: Scarecrow, 1976.

John and Anne Spear, *The Encyclopedia of Ghosts and Spirits.* London: Headline, 1992.

Philip Stander and Paul Schmolling, *Poltergeists and the Paranormal.* St. Paul, MN: Llewellyn, 1996.

G.N.M. Tyrell, *Apparitions.* New York: Collier Books, 1953.

Michael White, *Weird Science: An Expert Explains Ghosts, Voodoo, the UFO Conspiracy, and Other Paranormal Phenomena*. New York: Avon, 1999.

Colin Wilson, *Poltergeist: A Study in Destructive Haunting*. St. Paul, MN: Llewellyn, 1993.

## Haunted House Compilations

*Hundreds of books are available that recount reported encounters with ghosts. The accounts range from brief summaries to detailed accounts. Here is a small sampling:*

Hans Holzer, *More Where the Ghosts Are: The Ultimate Guide to Haunted Houses*. New York: Citadel, 2002. *See also many other books by this author.*

Michael Norman and Beth Scott, *Historic Haunted America*. New York: Tor, 2001. *See also other books by these authors.*

Frank Spaeth, ed., *Phantom Army of the Civil War and Other Southern Ghost Stories*. St. Paul, MN: Llewellyn, 1997.

## Ghostly Gazetteers

*There are dozens of "travel guides" that list and describe places you can visit where hauntings are said to have occurred. Here are a few examples:*

Dennis William Hauck, *The International Directory of Haunted Places*. New York: Penguin, 2000.

———, *The National Directory of Haunted Places*. 3rd ed. New York: Penguin, 2002.

Frances Kermeen, *Ghostly Encounters: True Stories of America's Haunted Inns and Hotels*. New York: Warner, 2002.

Robin Meade, *Haunted Hotels*. Nashville: Rutledge Hill, 1995.

## Websites

Borley Rectory, www.borleyrectory.com. Operated by Vince O'Neil, son of a prominent figure in the history of the Borley Rectory, "the most haunted house in England."

Committee for the Scientific Investigation of Claims of the Paranormal (CSICOP), www.csicop.org. CSICOP is the most prominent skeptical organization in the United States. The organization encourages critical thinking and skepticism about paranormal and other "fringe" topics.

Ghostcam Sites, www.courierpress.com/ghost, www.irelandseye.com/ghost/index.shtm, and www.bbc.co.uk/so/weird/cam. All have "ghostcams"—cameras that remain turned on twenty-four hours a day, providing a live still picture that is refreshed every thirty seconds or so (this might vary by site). All are set up at sites where ghosts have been reported frequently. The first is in the Willard Library, Evansville, Indiana, home of the famous "Gray Lady" ghost. The second is in a Belfast, Ireland, Victorian-era linen mill, where people report seeing the ghost of a sixteen-year-old cleaning girl. The third is in Llancaiach Fawr Manor in South Wales, reputedly one of the most haunted homes in Great Britain.

Haunted Places Directory, www.haunted-places.com. This website is operated by Dennis William Hauck, a notable ghost hunter and the author of *The National Directory of Haunted Places* and *The International Directory of Haunted Places*. It provides information about Hauck's ghost investigations, haunted tours, and related topics.

Prairie Ghosts, www.prairieghosts.com. Operated by Troy Taylor, a ghost investigator and author, this site is also the home of the American Ghost Society, an organization for ghost and haunting enthusiasts. The site contains extensive links and many articles on various topics related to ghosts and hauntings, both historical and contemporary.

The Skeptic's Dictionary, www.skepdic.com. This site presents a skeptical view of more than four hundred "strange beliefs, amusing deceptions, and dangerous delusions," including ghosts and hauntings.

# Index